Mirror Books *presents*

**The second crime for
the Cold Case Jury**

DEATH OF AN ACTRESS

After finishing this book,
readers are invited to deliver
their own verdicts at the
Cold Case Jury website
coldcasejury.com

ACKNOWLEDGEMENTS

I am indebted to Paul Stickler and the Hampshire Constabulary History Society for granting access to the full police files of the case. This book would not have been written without the help and support of my wife Carla, who offered plentiful edits, suggestions and discussions.

I wish also to thank:
Dr Mark Aley, Professor Jill Belch, Jim Brown, Gloria Dimick, Richard Latto and Dr Okosieme. Finally, a thank you to everyone at Mirror Books who helped put this book into your hands, especially Jo Sollis and Julie Adams.

COLD CASE JURY
TRUE CRIME COLLECTION

DEATH
OF AN ACTRESS

ANTONY M BROWN

Published by Mirror Books,
an imprint of Trinity Mirror plc,
1 Canada Square,
London E14 5AP, England

www.mirrorbooks.co.uk
twitter.com/themirrorbooks

ISBN 978-1-910335-82-6

First paperback edition

Printed and bound in Great Britain
by CPI Group (UK) Ltd, Croydon, CR0 4YY

CONTENTS

BEST SERVED COLD

I agree with George Orwell, who famously lamented the decline of the English murder. He thought original murders were virtually extinct by the first half of the 20th Century, and that brutality had replaced ingenuity in pursuance of the ultimate crime. Gone were the days of assiduous poisonings, carefully laid traps and mysterious killings without apparent motive. These were now the preserve of thrillers, movies and, of course, dear Aunt Agatha. Fact had lost its frisson to fiction and reality was left somehow diminished.

There is a quality to a bygone murder that seems to set it apart from its modern counterparts. It was an era of etiquette and arsenic, of afternoon tea with a spoonful of malice. Modern Britain is too open, too honest even, to create the social conditions of the past that drove some to commit murder, often with an insidious craft that flummoxed the authorities of the day.

This last point is important. Like revenge, a venerable murder is best served cold. Unsolved. These are the intriguing cases that have several plausible solutions and have bequeathed us enough evidence to let us debate what probably happened. These are the masterpieces of murder, to quote the title of an Edmund Pearson book, the dark art that would be hung upon the cold walls of a

Tate Criminal Gallery. These are the cases for the Cold Case Jury.

Does this mean that these crimes were perpetrated by the Machiavellis of murder? No, an unsolved crime from Orwell's golden age of murder does not imply its criminals were more deviously clever than today's. Undoubtedly some were, but the truth is that many of these cold cases would be solved by today's higher standards of professionalism and scientific methods of detection. Even the assassination of President Kennedy in 1963, arguably the most analysed murder of the last century, spawned a vast conspiracy-theory industry largely because of a flawed autopsy. Whether this was by malign influence or honourable incompetence is a quicksand best avoided here. My point is that, had the autopsy retrieved the bullet fragments from the President's brain, subsequent forensic analysis would have revealed the type of gun that terminated a presidency that bright November day and the shadows of doubt, as well as an industry, might have disappeared.

So, am I re-investigating these cold cases, unearthing fresh evidence, or presenting new theories to shed light on old crimes? Sometimes, yes, but my overriding goal is to present the reader with an interesting case for which the verdict is open to doubt. My task is to take the reader back in time to witness the events leading up to a violent or suspicious death; reconstruct how it occurred according to the different theories; and present evidence to the reader as in a real court. I hope to bring these crimes back to life, showing how the drama might have unfolded, emphasising the timeless interplay of the people involved and presenting the historical stage on which they acted. In reconstructing events I prefer to use narrative's present tense – dialogue. Some of it is verbatim, drawn from trial or inquest testimony. The rest is more a work of imagination, yet always governed by the facts and theories of the case, connecting the evidential dots by plausible lines of narrative.

I hope I am also an impartial advocate – the Cold Case Advocate, if you like. My aim is to show the strengths and weaknesses of each theory and then you have your say. I'm hoping you will give your verdict on the Cold Case Jury website. In time, an overall verdict of the Cold Case Jury will emerge for each case.

My final task is to present my views on the case. But my view is only one.

The verdict always lies with you, the jury.

Preface

PERSONAL CONNECTIONS

I have a personal connection to this case. The trial of James Camb was held in Winchester, the town in which I was born and still consider my home. The *Durban Castle*, the ship from which Gay Gibson disappeared, was part of the famous Union Castle Line that sailed weekly between Cape Town and Southampton, where I often looked seaward from the docks as a boy.

The case also pivots around the personal relationship between a first-class passenger and a deck steward. Was there a spark of attraction between them that led to intimacy and tragedy? Or was the steward a sexual predator who turned violent when his attentions were spurned?

Legally, the case was unusual because there was no body to prove cause of death. A conviction rested on circumstantial evidence. Many disagreed with the jury's verdict believing a sudden natural death was possible. Indeed, some believe it was more likely than murder. Having secured access to the full police files for the first time, which contain new evidence never before published, this absorbing case is another to put before the Cold Case Jury.

The result is in your hands.

Antony M. Brown, *December 2017*

ACT ONE

The Story

This is the true story of the death of
Gay Gibson in 1947.

It led to one of the most famous
British trials of the 20th Century.

Chapter 1

SUDDEN DEPARTURES

Southern Daily Echo, Saturday 25 October 1947
ACTRESS DISAPPEARS ON VOYAGE TO SOUTHAMPTON

Southampton CID officers spent several hours aboard the Union Castle liner Durban Castle *at Southampton today, making a thorough inspection of the first-class cabin occupied by a 21-year-old, auburn-haired London actress Miss Eileen (Gay) Gibson, who disappeared on the night of 17-18 October during the voyage from Cape Town. Miss Gibson was returning to this country after taking part in a stage show at Johannesburg.*

Gay Gibson went to her cabin shortly after midnight following a dance, which she had attended with the other first-class passengers. Early the next morning a stewardess went to the cabin with the morning tea, but Miss Gibson was missing. Captain Patey was informed. The liner was turned back whilst a search was made within and around the ship. When no trace of the young actress could be found, Captain Patey sent a radio signal to the London office of Union Castle Line asking the police to meet the ship because of "complications".

During the night, two CID officers took statements from two first-class passengers and three or four members of the crew, including a stewardess. All the articles and furniture in the missing woman's cabin – including the

3

bedstead and bedding, carpets and rugs – were removed from the cabin during the morning.

This morning the single-berth accommodation that Miss Gibson had occupied was barred and padlocked. A man came ashore accompanied by detectives, and was taken to Southampton Police headquarters for questioning.

*

When a local paper broke the story of Gay Gibson's disappearance it soon became headline news across the country. The sensational case provided a distraction from the bleak austerity of post-war Britain, where the euphoria of Victory in Europe had been replaced by the reality of continued rationing. This was reflected in the other lead story of the *Southern Daily Echo* that day – "Perils of Cold and Hunger", which was a phrase used by President Truman to highlight the mounting peacetime problems facing Western Europe. Little wonder that "60,000 cases of grapefruit on the way to Britain" was a headline jostling for space next to the "Actress Disappears" lead.

It was a different era to today, especially for travel. The sound barrier had been broken by Chuck Yeager less than a fortnight before, and the jumbo jet and package holiday were still decades away. For most people, long-distance travel, if undertaken at all, was by liner. For an aspiring actress returning to England, the two-week voyage on a ship such as the *Durban Castle* was the only option. This lavender-hulled liner was a vessel of the distinctive and much-loved Union Castle fleet, which regularly plied the route between England and South Africa, carrying tons of mail and thousands of passengers each year.

The disappearance story moved quickly and sensationally. On the following Monday, the Echo's lead story was "Missing Body Murder Charge at Southampton". It was reported that James

Camb, a deck steward on the *Durban Castle*, had been remanded in custody "on a charge of murder on the high seas". A little under five months later, he was tried in the imposing Great Hall of Winchester. Press interest, always high for a murder trial because conviction carried the death sentence, was almost frenzied. Indeed, Camb's experienced barrister would later write that, of all the 40 murder trials in which he was involved, none intrigued the public more or was generally as well remembered. Legally, the case was open to more doubt than usual because there was no body of the victim to provide vital clues to the guilt or innocence of the accused. The case centred largely on the testimony of Camb, the evidence found in the cabin and the character and health of Gay Gibson. After a dramatic four-day trial, Camb was found guilty and sentenced to hang.

Many consider there was insufficient evidence to convict. Julian Symons, a respected crime writer at the time, believed the guilty verdict was the least defensible of any contemporaneous murder trial. But if Camb was not guilty beyond a reasonable doubt, it leaves unanswered the most important question of all: what happened on that balmy night when the *Durban Castle* steamed over the equator off the coast of West Africa? Was the jury correct in thinking Camb was responsible for her death or were the deck steward's repeated claims that he did not murder the actress true all along?

Until now, the police case file has remained closed and never been seen by the public. For the first time, in this book, all the evidence will be examined and assessed. The definitive story can now be told as this extraordinary case is presented to you, the Cold Case Jury. In Act One, I will take you back in time, reconstructing how events unfolded, with different versions of how the young actress might have met her untimely end. Key points of evidence will be introduced and discussed. In Act Two, you will see original evidence – including statements of witnesses not called to the trial and reports of the investigating police officers. Finally, in Act Three, I present my view of the case. But you do not have to accept my judgement. It is your opinion that matters. As in a real court of law, the verdict always rests with you, the jury.

Before we examine the events that led to the death of the young actress, we must begin by establishing the health and character of Gay Gibson. Both of these factors were crucial issues at the trial of the man accused of murdering her, and will have an important bearing on your view of the case.

*

Our story begins in Jamalpur, a suburban town in the semi-arid corner of northeast India, tucked between the mountains of Nepal to the north and the plateaus of Bangladesh to the east. Famed for its locomotive workshop, its heyday was in the early decades of the 20th Century, when the East Indian Railway Company employed thousands to manufacture and repair steam engines. Since their skills commanded higher wages than at home, expatriate craftsmen and their families were drawn to Jamalpur. One of these workers was blacksmith Joseph Gibson and his wife, Ellen, affectionately known as Daisy. And it was here, just as the heavy rains of the monsoon season were about to begin, that their third child, Eileen, was born on 13 June 1926.

Five months later, the family returned to England. After only six months, Joseph accepted a position with the Burma Oil Company and returned to Asia, where he would remain until 1935. With her husband abroad, the iron-willed Daisy raised the three children according to her Baptist beliefs. However, it appears that Joseph was the most committed disciple, his spare time being devoted to the church and preaching wherever he was stationed. As a child, Eileen was dumpy and rather plain, but adolescence saw her lose some of the puppy fat. She was attractive rather than beautiful, sensible rather than academic. Reasonably athletic, she was a good swimmer and enjoyed hockey. She had a keen sense of the theatrical, and from quite an early age she told friends and family she wanted to be an actress.

In March 1939, Joseph took a position in Persia (now Iran) and a year later was joined by his wife and Eileen, who was educated by a private tutor. By June 1941, the political situation had become unstable due to the war, and mother and daughter were evacuated to England. On her return, according to a family friend, Daisy was proudly "telling everyone that Eileen had been very popular on the ship and had many proposals of marriage from the passengers". Clearly, 15-year-old Eileen looked and acted older than her age.

While in her mid-teens, Eileen participated in fundraising dances for local prisoners of war, and the spirited and enthusiastic teenager was one of "the gay young things" who stood out. The name stuck. Eileen became Gay Gibson, the glamorous actress of the West End and Broadway – or so she dreamed. Her theatrical pretentions were noticed. "She had become very affected, a changed person," a male friend remembered. "She dressed in the style of someone much older, a theatrical type, trying to create an impression of her talent and beauty on every possible occasion."

In the summer of 1944, 18-year-old Gay followed her mother's footsteps and began training as a nurse. Soon disillusioned with her choice of career, she left after only four months. In February 1945, as her mother was preparing to join her husband overseas, Gay joined the Intelligence Corps of the Auxiliary Territorial Service (ATS), the female section of the British Army. A natural linguist, she studied Japanese and expected to be posted to the Far East, but the end of the war forced a change of plan. She joined Stars in Battledress, a troupe of entertainers drawn from serving members of the armed forces that produced plays, revues and musical shows for the exclusive entertainment of the forces, home and abroad.

During the first half of 1946, Gay was busy performing the lead role in the play *The Man with a Load of Mischief*. After weeks of rehearsals in London, the production went on tour from April until August, including some shows in Germany. Peter Dalby, a professional stage manager before his call up, worked closely with her for several months, up to eight hours a day and sometimes sharing the same digs. He later testified that he found Gay hysterical, excitable, neurotic and prone to fits of crying, which went far beyond the typical temperamental excesses of an actress. He also recounted that she quickly became infatuated with an army driver called Pierre. She even had a cigarette burn on the back of her hand as a kind of improvised tattoo, something to remember him by. She claimed she was engaged to Pierre but broke it off when she realised her mistake.

In early July, Evelyn Armour, a junior ATS officer, was called out late one evening to see Private Gibson after she was reported ill. When she arrived Gay was laying on the bed face upwards, her back arched. Clutching her chest, her tongue was at the back of her throat and she appeared to be choking. An ambulance was called. Gay later informed Armour that she had experienced another "turn". Surprisingly, at least to modern medical practice, Gay was not referred to a specialist. Perhaps she wanted to play down the attacks. Certainly she did not tell her mother, who remained unaware of them until the trial.

In September, Gay began rehearsals for a minor role in *Jane Steps Out*, which went on tour from October until December. After one of the final shows, Dalby recalled, Gay had to be carried from an army lorry, apparently unconscious. The tour ended a week before Christmas 1946, and it was the last time Gay acted with the army troupe.

After India, Burma and Persia, Joseph Gibson's wanderlust next took him to work in South Africa, and it was decided his wife and Gay would join him there. The decision appeared rushed. In February 1947, to facilitate the move, Private Gibson was demoted to the ATS Reserves on compassionate grounds. As part of her active demobilisation she underwent a medical and was passed physically fit, with a crucial qualification: she was not to be stationed in the heat and humidity of the tropics due to a chronic ear infection. Indeed, two weeks previously, she had been admitted to hospital for six days with *otitis media*, an inflammation of the middle ear. The medical officer also observed that "she was a bit wheezy" and there were indications that "she had slight bronchitis". There was no record of any fits or convulsions. Before undertaking the two-week journey to South Africa on the *Carnarvon Castle*, Gay saw a doctor for depression.

On 12 March 1947, mother and daughter were met in Cape Town by Joseph Gibson and travelled overland to a rented bungalow in Durban. After only two weeks Gay left, the allure of acting pulling her to Johannesburg, where she was resident at Alledene boarding house for two months. She fainted at least once, telling a fellow guest she was worried about the state of her health and believed her "heart was affected".

Gay joined a repertory company, landing a part in its production of *The Silver Cord*, a Sidney Howard play, coincidentally written in the year of her birth. Its one-week run ended on Gay's 21st birthday. Like most 21-year-olds, she must have been excited about the future, stretching ahead of her like a highway disappearing over a distant horizon. But she had less than a hundred days to live.

Gay was now in her physical prime. She had perfect skin: unblemished and smooth, porcelain white, almost translucent. A male colleague remarked, "She had the most beautiful skin I have ever seen in my life: white, like alabaster. It was the most striking thing about her." But it wasn't her only striking feature. She had Bette Davis eyes, sensual lips and a bob of luxurious red hair that she would twirl for attention. Although many hesitated to describe her as beautiful, she was certainly attractive. A fellow actress recalled that she attracted men like bees to a honeycomb.

In July 1947, Gay landed the lead female role in *Golden Boy*, Clifford Odets' play about a young man torn between the material rewards of boxing and his love of music. In a made-to-measure part, the play also starred Eric Boon, a former British lightweight champion who had participated in the first televised boxing fight in 1939. Much of the evidence concerning Gay's behaviour is drawn from the experiences of the cast who worked with her for six weeks, in particular from the play's wispy-haired actor-producer Henry Gilbert, his elegant wife Ena Schoub, and swarthy-looking actor Mike Abel.

Henry Gilbert cast Gay in the play and initially found her "a charming, nice, well-behaved young lady". But, as the weeks passed, she was "often distraught, emotional and highly strung". She complained to him, he would later testify, that asthma forced her to stop taking her singing lessons. This is consistent with the recollections of Gay's singing teacher in Johannesburg. She recalled that her pupil failed to hit certain notes because of chest and throat trouble. When she examined Gay's mouth she was alarmed to see a yellow-headed lump at the back of her throat. Convinced it was tonsillar tuberculosis, she was relieved when Gay stopped taking lessons.

Towards the end of July, Gilbert introduced Gay to his wife, Dr Ena Schoub, a casualty officer at Johannesburg General Hospital. She described Gay as "a very nice, charming girl". Ena quickly became a friend in whom Gay could confide. Sometime in August, a worried Gay told the doctor that her period was two weeks late. Ena asked the young actress what contraceptive she was using, but Gay gave a blank look. It appears Gay was sexually active, but also naive. Ena told her a late period did not necessarily mean she was pregnant and advised Gay to fit a contraceptive diaphragm.

Rehearsals for *Golden Boy* began in early August. Actor Mike Abel was well cast: he had the look of the gangster he was playing. Gay told him, he would later testify, that she had no family: her parents had died during the Blitz and her brothers were killed in the Navy. Both statements were false. Either Gay was prone to lying for dramatic effect, or Abel was. His observation that Gay liked to drink at times was confirmed by others. Mike Abel and Gay must have hit it off quickly because, two weeks after they first met, Gay felt able to confide in him that she was pregnant. "She asked me for £200 to get to England to get a doctor to take care of her," Abel testified. He could not afford her request, which is not surprising because Gay had asked for today's equivalent of £7,500. When Abel asked who the father was, Gay laughed.

It might have been incredulous laughter. Doreen Mantle, best known for her portrayal of Jean Warboys in the sitcom *One Foot in the Grave*, also acted in *Golden Boy* and recalls a cast party: "At that party, I remember her having a big argument with Mike Abel, accusing him of making her pregnant, which was a big thing in those days. Nobody talked about these things. I was shocked." This explosive evidence was never heard at the trial. Doreen, then a 21-year-old social worker, did not travel to England for the trial, and Abel was hardly likely to admit to an extra-marital affair in court, only to see it splashed all over the South African newspapers for his wife to read.

This evidence raises a question that has significance in how later events are interpreted. Was Gay pregnant or was she fabricating the story, perhaps to buy her passage home to England?

If it was the latter, it was a desperate ruse because an unmarried mother was still widely shunned as a social pariah at this time.

Even if he was the father, the relationship with Mike Abel was short-lived. By the end of August, Gay was introducing a new boyfriend. Charles Schwentafsky was married, 33 years old, slightly built, clean-shaven and dark-haired. Born in Austria, the naturalised British citizen was in Johannesburg chasing a licence for aluminium manufacturing. After they had met in the Carlton Lounge, Gay and Charles were frequently seen in each other's company. He bought Gay clothes and regularly sent flowers.

As rehearsals progressed, the cast became concerned for Gay's health. On at least one occasion, the skin around her mouth and on her hands turned blue and she passed out. She also fainted at a cast party, on a busy street and in Mike Abel's car. Doreen Mantle remembered that "Gay had not been strong" and the cast were concerned she might not be able to carry on with the show.

Golden Boy opened at the Standard Theatre in Johannesburg on 10 September 1947 to largely positive reviews, although one critic remarked dryly that everyone was typecast. Gay's performance as Lorna Moon was described as "convincing", "sharply delineated" and played with "hardly a false note". Most plaudits went to Mike Abel who, it was unanimously agreed, stole the show as the gun-running hoodlum. Despite the good reviews, the play's three-week run was cut short ten days later when the theatre was closed by the municipality due to concerns over its fire certificate. Indeed, it was described as a "potential funeral pyre". The grand Victorian theatre never reopened and was demolished nine years later.

As soon as *Golden Boy* closed on the Saturday, Henry Gilbert hurriedly arranged for the play to transfer to Pretoria. However, before the cast moved north a second problem finished the play for good: Gay was in Gilbert's office on Monday morning asking to be released. She wanted to pursue her acting career back home, she said, and had letters of introduction, including one for the Abbey Theatre in Dublin. Even though he was sceptical about her motive, Gilbert tore up her contract and, with no time to find a new leading actress, cancelled the show. Gay had won her freedom, but had less than four weeks to enjoy it.

On 26 September, Gay and Charles checked into the Torquay Hotel in Durban, staying in adjoining rooms for four nights. When they left, Charles picked up the tab for both of them. A week later, he was at Stamford Aerodrome to see Gay board her flight to Cape Town. He later told police that he had given her over £500 in cash and traveller cheques – a huge sum, equivalent to the average annual salary in Britain at the time.

After two nights in Cape Town, Gay boarded the *Durban Castle* on 10 October for the two-week trip to Southampton. She soon told at least four people on the liner that she was crazily in love with Charles. In one letter to a male friend, written days before her departure, she says she felt very happy but, showing a prophetic pessimism, was worried it would end. If she was happy and in love, it is strange that she left Africa so suddenly and, even more unusually, that Charles would pay lavishly for it. Even if he was smitten, why would a wealthy businessman give so much money to a young woman he had known for only a few weeks?

Daisy Gibson later testified that the money was a loan to help launch her daughter's career in England. If this were the case, Charles knew he would never see Gay again, let alone his money. Businessmen never keep their wallets by their hearts. There is another possible explanation: Gay had told Charles she was pregnant, and he was persuaded to help. There would be little difficulty in convincing him that she was best taken care of in England, away from the censure of her mother and the puritanical wrath of her father. Gay would have known whether she was pregnant by the middle of September. If she had missed a second period, she could not attribute its absence to the effects of her exhausting work or Johannesburg's high altitude. The timing fits with her sudden departure from the play and the country.

Members of the Cold Case Jury, I suggest the testimony of Gay's colleagues paints the following picture. She was well-liked but prone to emotional outbursts and dramatic exaggeration; she had some health concerns; she liked the company of men and was sexually active, possibly pregnant. All of this was emphatically denied by Daisy Gibson. Even though mother and daughter lived apart for five of the six months Gay was in South Africa, Daisy was adamant she knew everything about her daughter. As far as she was concerned, there had been no drinking, no sex and no missed periods. But aren't these just the things any 21-year-old daughter would keep from the disapproving maternal eye? For a daughter living away from home, these secrets would not be difficult to hide. And certainly not for an actress.

Chapter 2

A MEMORABLE ENTRANCE

Having explored the character of Gay Gibson, as far as possible from the available evidence, we must now visit for the first time the decks of the *Durban Castle* to discover more about James Camb, the deck steward who would later be charged with her murder. The dramatic reconstructions in the following chapters not only demonstrate the character of Camb and his relationship with Gay, but also the chain of events that led to her death. They are based on the facts established at the trial, the original police reports and witness statements.

On Tuesday 7 October 1947, Gay Gibson returned to Durban for what would prove to be the final embrace of mother and daughter. The next morning, she flew to Cape Town. We pick up the story on Friday afternoon, when she boarded the *Durban Castle*.

*

3pm The face staring back from the mirror was rounded, of olive complexion, with brown, downturned eyes. Perhaps its most striking feature was the thin upper lip, grooved with a deep cupid's bow that highlighted the full-bodied one below. He swept his straight black hair from his forehead and carefully placed the peaked cap on his head. The first-class deck steward looked extraordinarily suave in his white deck uniform – a long-sleeved jacket buttoned up to the neck with white trousers – and regularly drew admiring glances from the female passengers, who often remarked on his resemblance to Tyrone Power, one of the day's leading actors. This always pleased James Camb, not least because it meant he could expect a higher-than-usual tip. He stepped out of the Long Gallery onto the wide walkways of Promenade Deck. This was his dominion.

In the centre of the deck was a series of social rooms exclusively for the enjoyment of first-class passengers. Moving sternwards, there was the lounge where passengers could relax with a drink to a piano accompaniment. Leading from this to the Smoke Room on the port side was a small library and the Long Gallery, its large bow window affording panoramic views of the ocean horizon when the ship was cruising. Opposite the Long Gallery on the starboard side were the bar and Deck Pantry. It was here that Camb would make up trays of sandwiches, afternoon tea or drinks from the bar, and deliver them to the passengers sunning themselves on deck or sheltering from the wind in the Long Gallery. From the Smoke Room one could reach the elegant veranda that overlooked the large outdoor swimming pool at the end of Promenade Deck. Less well-heeled passengers had to make do with the smaller swimming bath on B Deck.

Camb made his way to the railings near the front of Promenade Deck, affording himself a great view of Duncan Dock and the bustling city centre of Cape Town beyond. He never tired of seeing the majestic Cape skyline, dominated by jagged Devil's Peak on the left, framing the massive mesa of Table Mountain. He hadn't come to admire the view, however, but to watch the activity below. Since his promotion, he had made it a habit to watch passengers come aboard, carefully noting who came with the most luggage and had the most attendants fussing around them – an indicator of good tippers, he had quickly discovered.

After five minutes of watching the fret and bother of the elderly well-to-do, who always made up the bulk of the first-class passengers, he was joined at the rail by a plump colleague with the complexion of a boiled lobster. The two men exchanged a cursory nod of acknowledgement.

Camb broke the silence. His voice was quiet, well-spoken with a gentle Lancastrian accent. "There doesn't seem to be as many punters as usual."

"According to the manifest, we only have 60 first-class passengers this trip."

"That's less than half full."

"A little less than a third full, actually," the colleague remarked sanctimoniously.

"Blimey, it'll be like a ghost ship."

"There will still be plenty to do," the colleague cautioned, taking off his spectacles to clean them.

Camb's attention was drawn to the far end of the first-class gangway, where he caught sight of a swirl of auburn hair. A young woman, dark sunglasses contrasting with her milky complexion, a white stole flung around her shoulders and a bouquet of red roses in her hands, walked along the gangway with the poise of an actress on the red carpet at the Oscars. With a smile, she exchanged pleasantries with an older male passenger, and her vivacious giggle was carried to Camb on the light breeze. It was like a siren's song. Immediately transfixed, he watched her attentively as she glided down the gangway. "She's mine!" he proclaimed, slapping his right palm on the handrail, forgetting momentarily he had company.

"Better control yourself, Jim."

"Oh, I wager you would jump, given half a chance."

"You actually think you're God's gift, don't you?"

"I'll let you into a secret," Camb said, turning to face his colleague. "Unaccompanied first-class women are the easiest. It's the romance of the sea with no strings attached. They love our attention and deference. They know we have to be discreet. We're a far better option than getting involved with other passengers – that never ends well!" he laughed.

"Spare me the advice! Your entanglements hardly end well, do they?"

Ignored by Camb, who returned his attention to his quarry, the colleague pressed home his last point: "That girl on the last outbound?"

"Oh, she was a total tease," replied Camb nonchalantly. "Nothing happened. That was the problem. I put her over my knee and gave her a spanking for wasting my time."

"She was 16 years old, for God's sake, Camb! Mark my words – you're playing with fire. It's only a matter of time. One day you'll be reported or caught with your pants down in a passenger cabin. That's an immediate discharge; you'll never steward again."

"Yeah, everyone knows the score."

"And then your wife will find out about your little fun and games. Have you thought about that?"

"It's a wedding ring, not a ball and chain. What happens at sea, stays at sea. I love my family, whatever you may think." There was an uneasy silence, punctuated only by the shrieking of a lone gull soaring on the swirling gusts alongside the ship. Camb stepped on the lower railing and leaned forward, allowing him to watch the redhead until she disappeared into the first-class entrance hall below. He straightened up and, revealing his sense of anticipation, patted the handrail with both hands in a drum roll.

Sensing the increasing antipathy of his colleague, Camb turned to face him. "Look, I see it as a perk of the job, nothing more. But if you don't want to take advantage of it," he shrugged his shoulders, "well fine, that's up to you, but don't criticise me for getting some while I can. You never know when it will be your last."

Two decks below, Gay Gibson entered the first-class entrance hall on B Deck, which was adjacent to the spectacular open ceiling of the dining room on the deck below. Gay handed a smartly dressed steward her ticket.

"Welcome aboard, Miss Gibson," said Reginald Boothby. "I'm your cabin steward for the voyage. My job is to ensure you have a comfortable trip. If I'm not mistaken, I think you came aboard to inspect your cabin when we were docked at Durban?"

"Yes, with my mother," she replied, impressed that he had remembered her. Although with her striking looks, most men did.

"I trust it was to your liking?"

"Oh, yes."

"Did you have a good trip from Durban?"

"Yes, but I'm tired."

"Then I will not detain you much longer. I have a cablegram for you." He handed over a slip of paper. Gay felt a little emotional when she read the typed message: "Bon Voyage and God bless you – Mum and Dad."

"And this is Eileen Field, your stewardess during the voyage."

After the usual pleasantries, the prim and petite stewardess ushered Gay down the portside corridor, which felt more like a hospital than a luxury liner. There was a pungent smell of new paint and floor polish, not dissimilar to antiseptic; overhead, ducts and cabling jostled for space; and halfway down the long corridor there was a retractable meshed gate, the type Gay had seen in elevators, separating tourist and first-class cabins.

"Travelling back home?" the stewardess enquired.

"Yes, I'm hoping to pursue my stage career in Dublin. The timing could be better, though. I've just fallen head over heels!"

"And your boyfriend is staying in South Africa?"

"Yes, that's the problem. Well, it's not the only one," she added chirpily. "He's married, too!"

Field was shocked that the passenger was so loquacious with intimate details. She noted that Gay seemed untroubled by the fact she was in love with a married man.

"But I know he loves me!" Gay continued. "He's estranged from his wife, really. She lives in England. He's a successful businessman in Africa. It's a long story." Field said nothing. It sounded complicated and she feared things might not end well for her young passenger.

"It looks like I'm on the right deck," Gay joked, pointing to the signs for the hairdresser and the shop.

"They are at the end of this corridor on the right," Field confirmed. She also pointed out the location of several bathrooms as they walked by. "This way please, madam," the stewardess motioned and turned sharp right. Gay followed her into a smaller, dimly lit alleyway that contained two doors on either side. The door furthest on the right, which bore the number 126, was opened. "Here you are."

Gay walked into the cabin, which was almost a perfect eight-foot cube. It was smaller than she remembered – a large man with outstretched arms could stand in the middle and almost touch both walls. Opposite the door, in the corner of the room, was a fitted wardrobe. To her left, by the outside wall, was a metal-framed bed on which her suitcase was already lying, waiting for her. The stewardess pointed to the wall above the bed. "The porthole opens inwards and upwards. You need to fasten it to the wall with the catch. It's quite awkward, so please call if you want it opened, but we recommend you keep it closed until we reach the tropics." She then pointed to a series of three buttons in a panel halfway up the wall between the bed and a chest of drawers tucked into a recess by the door. "Push the bottom one to summon me, the middle for a steward. If you press either after 10pm the nightwatchman will respond."

"And the switch at the top?"

The stewardess flicked it. The semi-cylindrical light above the panel came on. "Your bedside light." It was promptly turned off again.

"Does the door have a lock?" Gay inquired.

"There's a bolt here," replied the stewardess, pointing to the door, "although we do not advise you to use it, Miss Gibson. It's really not necessary for security and could be dangerous in case of emergency. I think we're all set, don't you? If you need anything, don't hesitate to call. On behalf of Captain Patey, we hope you have a pleasant voyage." The stewardess quickly withdrew, the door closing behind her with a click.

Gay unzipped her large brown suitcase. Most of her clothes and shoes went into the wardrobe, including her favourite silver shoes and a lemon quilted dressing gown with a full-length zip at the front. She put her folded black silk pyjamas on the bed, and hung an elegant black evening dress on a hook on the far wall. On top of the small chest of drawers she placed an alarm clock, green hairbrush and vanity bag. All of these personal effects were unremarkable, but all would play a role in the denouement of a fatal drama. Some would never be found, others would be exhibited before a packed courtroom in one of the most sensational trials of the century. And in the dock accused of her murder would be the good-looking steward, now busily serving drinks and sandwiches above her on Promenade Deck.

*

Members of the Cold Case Jury, having glimpsed 30-year-old James Camb on the decks of the *Durban Castle*, you have seen how his conceit and attitude towards women alienated some of his colleagues. Indeed, his cabin antics were so well known by other crew members that he was nicknamed "Don Jimmy", alluding to the womaniser of legend, Don Juan. The reference to the 16-year-old girl in the reconstruction is based on claims made after Camb was arrested and these will be examined later. For now, we need to know more about the deck steward.

James Camb was born on 16 December 1916 in Waterfoot, a small mill-town tucked among the rolling Pennine hills of southeast Lancashire, to Bob Camb, a shoe factory worker, and his wife, Lillie. Just over two months later, Lillie tragically died, leaving James to grow up without the love of a mother. No child can be left untouched by such a tragedy, and while the precise effects will vary greatly from one individual to the next, they always run deep.

He was raised by his father and an aunt. Even as a boy, James was something of a smooth operator: well turned out, charismatic, quick-witted and a good talker, fluent in charm and persuasion. These were traits that would be refined in adulthood, especially in the company of women. He was also polite and courteous, at least when he wanted to be. On other occasions he showed an antagonising narcissism that strained relationships, especially with other boys. To his school friends, he appeared bright and should have performed better at school, but he was undisciplined, unruly and mischievous. Indeed, he appears to have had a justified reputation for being disruptive and provoking trouble, traits that maturity would not ameliorate.

On finishing his education at 14 years old, he worked for J. H. Hirst, a local slipper factory. Camb's energy and ambition soon eclipsed the mediocrity of his provincial life. He feared his future was all too clearly reflected in the dour faces of the men who traipsed from the mills and slipper factories to the working men's club. They appeared trapped in soulless marriages to local girls whose aspirations culminated in a family holiday to Morecambe. He would not be the butterfly broken upon the industrial wheel.

He yearned for adventure, excitement and, from a young age, the romance of the open sea, with its unbounded horizon and sense of timeless freedom.

At 16, James Camb realised his boyhood dream when he joined the crew of the *Rotorua*, but his enthusiasm at signing-on was short-lived. Spending months at sea ferrying thousands of tons of butter and wool between England and New Zealand was not his idea of life on the high seas. Looking dashing in a uniform was idle if there were no pretty girls to impress. He soon left the dreariness of the *Rotorua*, perhaps fortuitously, as it was sunk by a U-boat in 1940.

During the Second World War, Camb joined the Merchant Navy Reserve, spending his time on various ships, although the most significant event during this time happened onshore. In September 1943, after a short romance during leave, he married Margaret McCombie. The next year their daughter Evelyn was born. By this time Camb was back on the boats, seeing little of his wife and young daughter.

After the war, he returned to civilian life, becoming a machine operator in the Singer sewing machine factory at Clydebank. For someone who craved the adventure and romance of the sea, it was doomed to failure. Five months later, in April 1946, he joined the Union Castle fleet, which continuously ferried passengers, mail and cargo between Southampton and South Africa. He started his career as assistant cook on the *Durban Castle* and, a year later, through hard work and his general popularity with passengers, was promoted to deck steward first-class: a plum job. The hours were long but the duties were not onerous: serving drinks and snacks, attending to the comforts and whims of the older passengers, and overseeing subordinates to position the deckchairs and arrange deck games. Tips could be generous, especially for someone with insouciant charm and film-star looks. Camb could expect to double his basic salary, enough to lavish presents on his wife and daughter whenever he returned home.

But spending time at home was mere punctuation in the life of James Camb. His first love was the adventure of the sea and, most of all, romance on the decks. He had a reputation for darting in and out of female passengers' cabins, with a penchant for young women travelling alone. He was happy to indulge any physical pleasures if they desired, and was persistent if they did not. Although he had escaped an official reprimand, his behaviour had landed him in trouble before. It would do so again, but this time he would be forced to face the consequences.

Chapter 3

INTIMATE CONVERSATIONS

Camb's thoughts were far from home at 4pm on Friday 10 October, as the *Durban Castle* edged away from the quayside at Duncan Dock to begin its two-week voyage to Southampton. He was looking forward to the inevitable first encounter with the glamorous young woman with the auburn hair. It did not take long.

We return to the *Durban Castle* on the morning of Saturday 11 October, with the ship making steady progress off the western coast of southern Africa.

*

11am Gay Gibson first saw the dark-haired steward when he breezed in from the Promenade Deck through the double doors that separated the library from the Long Gallery. Average height, muscular, and dressed in his smart uniform, he soon disappeared from view as he walked into the bar. It had only been a glimpse, but Gay sensed a confidence in his poise and manner that aroused more than idle curiosity.

James Camb soon appeared again, carrying two tartan blankets in his arms. From her position by the window in the far corner of the Long Gallery, she tracked the dashing steward as he stepped outside on deck. A gust of wind ruffled his hair, which he immediately swept back. He approached two elderly ladies sitting in deck chairs. Gay estimated they were in their late 60s or early 70s. By their clothes, jewellery and superior air, she also surmised that they were moneyed. She could not hear the conversation but observed their delighted faces when Camb stooped, placing a blanket on each of their laps and tucking it around their legs. Their grateful reaction suggested that neither had requested the extra layer of warmth but that it had been brought by a steward who knew that, on a southern spring day at sea, the wind would have an edge to it.

For the next 15 minutes Gay lost sight of the steward. The book on the table held no interest for her and, as she had found at dinner the previous night, neither did the humdrum conversation of the other passengers, who appeared either old or ancient to a vivacious 21-year-old. She already feared that the two-week voyage was going to seem much longer. Her attention returned to Camb as he entered the Long Gallery, taking orders for drinks. She noticed he worked his way methodically from the front of the narrow room, engaging in conversation with each passenger. He approached a middle-aged woman sitting alone at a table near Gay. She was plastered with foundation and the blue eyeshadow served only to draw attention to the puffy bags under her eyes.

"How are you finding the *Durban Castle*, madam?"

"Everything is most satisfactory," she replied in a stony English accent.

"I'm very pleased to hear that," Camb said. "What can I get you to drink?"

"A gin and tonic, I think."

With a twinkle in his eye, he asked: "And what will your boyfriend have?" The woman's face lit up with a smile. The small talk continued a little longer before he left to return with a generous gin and tonic, which also pleased the passenger. Gay was in no doubt that her considerate steward was actually a smooth operator. If anything, it made him more interesting.

On entering the Long Gallery, Camb had immediately recognised the young redhead sitting alone at the small table in the corner. Despite the rush of adrenalin pulling him towards her, he had forced himself to pay attention to the other passengers first. Now, at last, she had motioned to him and he could approach her.

"Can I get you anything, madam?"

Gay leaned forward, tucking her legs under the chair and placing her hands on her knees. She tilted her head to one side slightly. Putting the slender cigarette holder to her lips, she inhaled, all the time looking at the attentive steward. She exhaled slowly, directing a plume of smoke towards Camb. "What can you offer me?" she asked, smiling.

"A drink from the bar, perhaps?"

"That sounds good," she cooed. "What do you have?"

"What do you like?" Camb smiled, already warming to his game.

"It's quite a long list," she giggled self-consciously, flicking the end of her cigarette into the glass ashtray on the table. "I like rum, but normally in the evening."

"Well, perhaps you could start your evening early?"

"No, I don't think so," she laughed.

"Pimm's?"

"I want something a bit more exciting," she countered. "Something to cheer me up, I think."

"Oh? Why would someone like you need cheering up?"

"That's a long story." Gay hesitated, averting her gaze.

Sensing the conversation was becoming too personal too quickly, Camb asked: "How about a cocktail? The bar has a shaker and I know how to make quite a few."

"Why not? A John Collins, please."

Camb spun on his heel and disappeared into the bar. As far as he was concerned, things could not have begun any better. She was more beautiful than he had hoped. He was certain that she was attracted to him, and they were only one day into the voyage. The "long story" sounded like boyfriend trouble. If he played his hand well, he would be in her cabin in a matter of days.

Camb returned, holding a tray aloft with the palm of his right hand, his left tidily tucked behind his back. As he placed the cocktail glass carefully onto the drink mat in front of her, he observed the spark in her beautiful brown eyes.

"A John Collins, madam. Enjoy," he said, bowing theatrically.

Gay giggled and took a sip. "That's perfect. Thank you." She replaced the glass on the table, which gently moved up and down with the swell, as if the ship were breathing.

"So, you're returning from holiday?" Camb asked, eager to restart the conversation.

"No, I've just finished performing in a play in Johannesburg – *Golden Boy*. Have you heard of it?" Camb shook his head. "Well, my leading man was Eric Boon. I bet you've heard of him."

"Yes, of course, the Thunderbolt. He's a good boxer."

"He's also an actor, you know. He's already been in a film, *Champagne Charlie*." The steward looked blankly. "With Tommy Trinder and Stanley Holloway?" Gay could see he was still none the wiser. "Well, I guess he brought some star quality to the production, being famous 'n' all."

"Is the play coming to London? I could come and see it when I get some leave."

"No, it finished early. It received good reviews and everything, but they closed the theatre."

"Sounds like tough luck. What will you do now?"

"I've got some introductions to theatres back home." She took another sip of her cocktail.

"And your boyfriend's joining you later?" Camb asked cheekily, although his only interest in the answer was to assess her likely availability.

"Charles has to run his business, so he couldn't come with me, but I can't stop thinking about him." She placed both her hands across her breast. "We've been going steady for only a month, but I'm already crazy about him. He's taken me to all the best restaurants and clubs in Johannesburg, you know."

Camb was not deterred by her proclaimed affection, but her answer seemed a little odd. "Why not stay and act in South Africa, then?" he asked.

"Well…" Gay hesitated, glancing down to the table. She took another sip of her drink. "Things are a little delicate right now."

"You mean he doesn't feel the same way?"

"No, he's crazy about me, too. I just know he is," she gushed.

"Well, if you were my girl, I wouldn't let you go," he joked. Camb expected a giggle in response but instead Gay suddenly looked pensive.

"It's just…" she started, taking a puff of her cigarette. "Well, let's just say, things may have become a little… complicated."

Camb asked jocularly, "You don't mean to tell me you're having a baby?"

Gay didn't take offence at Camb's familiarity. "Well, it's rather too soon to know," she replied cautiously.

"If that's the position, why don't you marry the man?"

There was a long pause. "It's not quite as easy as that."

"The longer you leave it…"

"He's already married," she cut in.

Camb said nothing, as he surmised the probable purpose of her trip to England. Gay changed the subject, her mood brightening a little as she spoke. "I'm going to have a rest after lunch. I always feel a little sleepy then. Would you mind bringing me a tray of afternoon tea in my cabin? At about four o'clock?"

"I cannot leave the Promenade Deck, especially at that time," Camb explained. "I'm busy with the tea service. When you want afternoon tea, summon the cabin steward and tell him what you want. I'll prepare your tray and he will bring it to your cabin."

Gay nodded as a male voice called out, "Steward, is it possible for someone else to get served here?"

"You'd better go," she smiled.

Camb slid a printed Manila slip and a stubby pencil across the table. "Could you sign and date it. You settle your account at the end of each week." Gay filled out the docket. "And your cabin number, please." He took the slip and circled five pence in the top corner, although he was more interested in knowing the cabin number. He said goodbye, and promptly left. The next time he looked into the Long Gallery there was only an empty, lipstick-marked cocktail glass on the corner table.

For the deck steward, the day progressed much like any other, except his thoughts kept returning to the young actress with the Bette Davis eyes. He did not have long to wait before a second encounter.

3:45pm As Camb was busily making up trays of afternoon tea to serve to passengers on Promenade Deck, a cabin steward stormed into the Deck Pantry. "What have you been telling Miss Gibson in 126?" he demanded angrily.

Camb was taken aback at the accusing tone. "Nothing," he replied defensively.

"Did you agree to take an afternoon tea to her cabin at four o'clock? You know damn well that deckies are not allowed in passenger cabins. Especially you!"

"I said I would prepare a tray for her. That's all."

"Why? You know that afternoon tea is served only on Prom Deck."

"She's had a rough time. I felt sorry for her."

"Funny how you always feel sorry for the young, pretty ones, isn't it?"

Camb ignored the barbed comment. "What did you say to her?"

"I said, given the circumstances, I would deliver the afternoon tea to her cabin this once, but apparently that's not good enough!" he glowered. "She's insisting you deliver it."

Camb tried to hide a faint smile of satisfaction. "I've already told her I can't do that. She must have misunderstood or something." Camb began to prepare a tray for tea service. "I had no intention of delivering it, honest. If she's really as insistent as you say, how about we both take it down?" As his colleague considered the compromise for a moment, Camb closed the deal: "Then I can explain the situation to her again."

"All right," his colleague sighed. "But only this once, you understand."

*

Members of the Cold Case Jury, let us step back a moment and take stock of the unfolding situation. Given this was the late 1940s, when social norms were more restrained, it is surprising that Gay would confide so quickly to complete strangers. Camb testified at the trial that his earliest conversation with Gay took place on either "the first day out or the second" from Cape Town. From the signed bar slip, we know it was the second day, Saturday 11 October. Not only does the conversation imply that the actress and steward were friendly from the outset, it also suggests that Gay had an easy-going intimacy towards men, something that was also alleged by Mike Abel and Henry Gilbert.

Was there already a spark of attraction between them? And did it ignite physical passion? Or was everything rather more innocent and amplified in the mind of a narcissist?

Chapter 4

GHOST SHIP

Gay Gibson settled quickly into a daily routine. She rose at 7:30am, when Eileen Field knocked on her cabin door to deliver an orange juice. At 8am she took her morning bath and an hour later she breakfasted. She usually spent the morning reading. After lunch, she often snoozed in her cabin before taking her tea tray prepared by James Camb. In the evening she would dine in the first-class restaurant. There were two other passengers on her allotted table – Mr Frank Hopwood, a procurement manager for the Union Castle Line, and William Bray, a squadron leader in the RAF. Both men were in their mid-40s and travelling alone on the liner, and they took a fatherly interest in the young woman. Hopwood escorted Gay to her cabin each night. With few other passengers about, Gay's corridor was eerily quiet, which made her a little anxious. She always bolted the cabin door behind her, despite being advised to the contrary.

On Monday 13 October, Gay wrote her last letter home {see *Exhibit 10*}. She remarked that the *Durban Castle* was like "a ghost ship" and that she spent most of the day dozing. Although not named, Hopwood and Bray were described as "very congenial table companions". She commented that on Tuesday evening there would be the first of three dances during the voyage. Gay would only live long enough to attend two.

We now turn our attention to Tuesday 14 October 1947.

*

5pm With a rapid snapping of heels on the wooden deck, Eileen Field turned into the Deck Pantry. "Here's the tray with compliments from Miss Gibson," she announced, placing the tray of empties on the cluttered counter.

Camb had his hands in the sink, washing up. "Did she send her compliments?"

"It's just a figure of speech."

"She's such a nice girl, isn't she?"

"And happily in love," Field retorted, almost as a warning to the womanising deck steward.

"Did you know Miss Gibson is three months pregnant by a married man?"

The stewardess was taken aback by the casual way the steward introduced such an inappropriate matter. Although Gay had happily told her that she was involved with a married man, she did not believe her passenger would have also said something of such an intimate nature to the steward. "You shouldn't go round saying things like that about a young lady."

"But Miss Gibson told me that herself."

Field suspected that the steward and the actress might be rather too familiar. Considered unprofessional and distinctly discouraged, it was risky for a crew member to become involved with a passenger. "It's dangerous to repeat the things passengers say," she added. "I would just busy yourself here, if I were you." She spun on her heels and was gone.

9:30pm By the veranda on Promenade Deck, the ensemble of musicians was playing a lilting waltz. A few passengers were moving slowly on their feet for the final dance, but most remained seated in the scattering of wicker chairs. As he played his violin, 48-year-old George Lovett was absorbed by the behaviour of the passengers at the table closest to the band, where a young woman was seated with two older companions. He recognised one was Frank Hopwood. Since the three sat down, the atmosphere had been tense.

Looking out to sea, Gay's body was angled away from her companions, occasionally giving a hard stare to each. She appeared agitated and emotional. As he continued to play, Lovett turned to the drummer. "Hey, Jack?" he whispered discreetly.

The drummer cocked his head in the direction of his band member. "What d'yer say?"

"There's some sort of quarrel going on." He pointed his violin in the direction of the table. "I think she's about to burst into tears."

Hopwood outstretched his hand in a gesture of reconciliation, but Gay was not looking. Bray tugged gently at her sleeve and she turned and listened, nodding slowly as he spoke. After Bray had finished, she stared at Frank Hopwood and, after an uncomfortable delay, finally shook his hand.

"I'd love to know what's going on," Lovett remarked.

When the band finished playing, Camb strode over to the musicians with a tray of drinks. "These are from Mr Hopwood." He placed the drinks on a table. Lovett placed his violin in its case and picked up his whisky.

Camb stood, staring at the three passengers. "She's only 21 and three months gone."

"Who?" asked Lovett.

"Who do you think?" Camb replied, gesturing with his eyes towards Gay, the only young woman present. In fact, she was the only young woman travelling first class.

"How do you know?" asked the drummer, overhearing the conversation.

"I've seen her identity card."

"It told you she's three months gone!"

"The things they put on identity cards these days!" another quipped. "It'll be inside leg measurements next!"

10:45pm In cabin 126, Gay pressed the red button in the middle of her bedside panel, ringing a bell outside the first-class pantry on A Deck, almost directly below her cabin. Nightwatchman Fred Steer, a gaunt-looking man with a viciously hooked nose and receding hair that made him appear far older than his 39 years, was reading a magazine. After finishing his page, he put it down and sauntered into the adjoining first-class dining room. He shuffled up the two flights of steps that led to the first-class entrance on B Deck, known as "The Square".

Steer turned right to look at the indicator board on the wall. It signalled that a bell had been rung from a portside cabin. He walked down the port corridor, glancing upwards, searching for an illuminated light outside one of the four alleyways that each led to a cluster of four cabins. Seeing it, he turned into the third alleyway, and on the far wall the red bulb for cabin 126 was illuminated. He pushed the bulb and the trail of lights he had followed was extinguished. It was an unwieldy system, but this is how a nightwatchman was summoned to a passenger's cabin.

Steer knocked. The bolt was slid back and the door opened cautiously. "You called for a steward?" he asked diffidently.

"Please could you ask the deck steward for my supper tray?" Gay asked.

"Yes, madam."

The door closed. When Steer arrived in the Long Gallery, he quickly found Camb. "Can you prep the tray for Miss Gibson? She's asking for it." The deck steward quickly prepared a pot of tea and sandwiches in the Deck Pantry. As Steer took the tray to cabin 126, he noticed there were two cups and saucers. He had not seen a visitor with Gay, but thought that Bray or Hopwood might be taking late-night tea with the actress, something they later denied. The identity of the other tea drinker was never discovered.

*

Members of the Cold Case Jury, two of the crew verified that, just a few days after the *Durban Castle* had departed Cape Town, James Camb told them that Gay Gibson was "three months gone". There is no evidence that any other crew member knew Gay might be pregnant, so either Camb invented the story or Gay told him. His remarks are consistent with the stories from Johannesburg, where Gay told at least two people she might have been pregnant. Also, the timing fits; it suggests the possible conception occurred in July. It is reasonable to assume the deck steward was telling the truth, particularly as he had little to gain from fabricating such a personal story. But what about the actress? Did Gay really believe she was pregnant, or was she merely trying to gain attention?

During the next few days, as the *Durban Castle* sailed north at a steady 18 knots, nothing significant occurred. Gay's routine continued. She became friendlier with her two dining companions. She told them on several occasions she was madly in love with Charles. This was no secret, nor did she hide the fact he was married. With his wife living in England, Charles Schwentafsky had an opportunity for independent living – and loving.

According to the companions, Gay's two loves in her life were pulling her in different directions. She was torn between staying in South Africa with her lover or returning to England to further her acting career. Intriguingly, according to Hopwood's revealing police statement {see *Exhibit 6*}, this dilemma was not resolved when she boarded the *Durban Castle*. Bray believed she was pensive and agitated about making her mind up. Which begs the question: why was she travelling to England? If it was related to a pregnancy, she never mentioned it around the dining table to the two men.

Hopwood also provided insight into her health. Worried that she was suffering from "heart trouble", Gay refused to participate in deck games. He also said Gay appeared tired, worried and "rather depressed at times". On several occasions Gay had "muddy coloured" fingernails, although Bray remembered them as bluish. She said it was due to bad circulation and that she might need injections for a "weak chest". Her dining companions on the liner confirmed much of what was said by her fellow actors in South Africa.

We now return to Promenade Deck on Friday 17 October 1947. The *Durban Castle* is 200 miles off the coast of Sierra Leone, having crossed the equator earlier that day. It is a hot, humid night. The temperature stubbornly refuses to drop below 80°F and there is little breeze to relieve the heat. The second dinner dance of the voyage has ended and Gay is sitting with her two companions in the first-class Smoke Room on Promenade Deck. She has less than four hours to live.

11:10pm "You were the belle of the ball, Miss Gibson," complimented the squadron leader. "Your silver shoes lit up the whole deck." Bray placed his glass on the circular table in the centre of the three armchairs occupied by the dining companions.

"Why don't we go for a swim?" Gay said, who had observed a steady procession of first-class passengers with swimsuits making their way through the Smoke Room to the swimming pool. "It's so dreadfully hot."

"You have a swim. We're happy to wait here," Bray suggested after conferring with Hopwood.

"All right," replied Gay, rising from her chair. "I need to fetch my swimsuit. Please excuse me." The two gentlemen also stood up.

"Shall I accompany you?"

"I'll be fine, Mr Hopwood. Thank you." As she left, dressed in an elegant black dress that highlighted her curvaceous figure, she drew discreet glances from many of the men. She walked confidently into the Long Gallery.

"I have a bone to pick with you," pronounced a stern voice. She stopped and turned to see James Camb standing behind her, smiling impishly. "And a big one at that," he added, his smile broadening.

"And what would that be?" she replied, puzzled.

"You did not use your tea tray last night, nor this evening. I had them prepared, as usual."

"Oh, there was nothing wrong with the tea service. After drinking the rum last night I didn't feel like having tea. It was too hot, anyhow. And this afternoon, I dozed off."

"And tonight?"

"I would like another rum, please. I really must dash," she said, turning to leave. "I need my swimsuit."

Back in her cabin on B Deck, she lifted her suitcase onto the bed, unzipped it and started to rummage through its contents. It was not long before she was disturbed by a knock on the door. She opened it halfway and was surprised to see Camb. "Oh? I didn't think you were allowed down here?" she remarked pleasantly. She pulled opened the door and resumed her search. "I cannot find my swimsuit anywhere. I know I packed it. Anyway, what can I do for you?"

"I wondered if you would like some lemonade with your rum."

"It's a long way to come just to ask me that," she laughed. "I don't, thank you."

There was an awkward silence before Camb asked: "Do you know what?"

Gay straightened up and faced him. "What?"

"I've got a good mind to get a drink and join you later."

"Please yourself," she said nonchalantly, her mind preoccupied by her missing swimsuit. "It's up to you," she added, opening the wardrobe door.

"I'd better get back now," he said quietly. "Otherwise I might be missed." On his return, Camb immediately poured a large glass of rum and placed it on the "bottle box", a ledge on the wall opposite the bar from where guests could collect drinks and return empties.

The bar closed at 11:30pm each night, but the dinner dance and the hot night meant that many first-class passengers were still milling about Promenade Deck and the closing-time routine was later than usual. Camb collected the empties from the bar and the Long Gallery, and took them to the pantry for washing-up.

11:35pm "I can't find it," Gay said, returning to her two companions. "It must be in my trunk in the hold."

"Never mind," said Hopwood. "They're closing the Smoke Room now. Shall we move outside?"

"Well, at least it might be a bit cooler out there."

"I doubt it," Bray commented. "It's so hot in the tropics."

The three stepped outside onto the starboard side of Promenade Deck. Above them stars were strung across the night sky; below the water crashed against the hull as the liner ploughed its way through the black ocean.

12:40am Bill Pott, a cabin mate, put his head round the door of the Deck Pantry. "Want a hand?"

"I'm all right, thanks," replied Camb, his hands in the tiny soap-filled sink, washing glasses.

"It's no bother, really. It's still too hot to turn in."

"I'll be finished soon enough. Go and have a smoke or something. I'll see you later."

Heading for his quarters, Pott ambled down Promenade Deck. He noticed Gay Gibson standing against the railing, talking to Frank Hopwood and William Bray.

12:45am "Goodnight," Bray said to his two companions as they reached the bottom of the stairs on B Deck. "See you tomorrow. Well, later today, actually." He turned right and headed towards his cabin. Hopwood and Gay turned left, walking the short distance to cabin 126. The shipping official entered Gay's quarters first and turned on the cylindrical light by the bed. "Sweet dreams," he said as he departed.

Gay thanked him and was hit by a wall of stultifying heat as she entered. There was no relieving breeze in the breathless cabin, even with the small porthole open. It was too uncomfortable for bed, she decided. The thought of the cooler temperatures on Promenade Deck was tempting. It would also be a pleasant change to shake off the chaperones, and she suddenly remembered she had not collected her glass of rum. That settled it. She placed a cigarette in her holder, lit it and, taking her alarm clock from the top of the drawers, headed out for a breath of night air and a little bit of rum and freedom.

When she reached Promenade Deck she headed for the bar. On a ledge on the right-hand side, and only a yard from the pantry where James Camb was washing up, she saw her glass of rum. She placed the clock on the ledge; she would collect it later. With her drink, she walked to the aft end of the deck near the first-class swimming pool. Leaning against the railing she looked up and lost herself again in the wonder of the night sky.

A few minutes later the solitude was shattered. "You'll have to move, miss, unless you want your pretty shoes to get soaked." William Conway, the boatswain's mate, was standing next to her, holding a mop. Behind him several men were swabbing down the deck.

"It's so hot down below. I thought I would come here for some fresh air. Not that there's much breeze, is there?"

"No, miss. We're in the tropics. It's a very warm and still night, I'm afraid."

"Well, I don't want to go back to my cabin. It's stifling, even with the porthole open."

"I suggest you move down amidships." Conway pointed to

where he meant. "We've already washed down there."

He paid little attention as Gay drifted towards the Long Gallery, her body sensing the constant shudder as the ship engines powered through the water. Standing on deck on a tropical night with the stars above, Gay's surroundings and her destination could not have formed a greater contrast. She was returning to the cold and rain, to ration books and queues, to the gloom of post-war austerity Britain.

On her arrival in a week's time, she planned to take the boat-train connection from Southampton to London. After that, arrangements were hazy. She had cabled the Cumberland, a popular choice of hotel with people travelling from South Africa, hoping to stay there for a few days. Before she left Durban, she wrote to a friend asking if she could stay with her, but nothing was certain. Apart from her fate, perhaps. The young actress would not live to see daybreak.

Chapter 5

MISSING

The following reconstruction is based on the captain's log and police statements of passengers and crew. It is early morning on Saturday 18 October 1947.

6am There was a knock on the cabin door. Punctual as ever, Eileen Field was dressed and ready for her duties, but any visitor to her cabin was unusual, especially at such an early hour. She opened the door to the senior nightwatchman.

"Sorry to bother you, Miss Field."

"Is there a problem, Mr Murray?"

"No, but we think Camb was in one of your passenger's cabins last night." He lowered his voice. "Cabin 126."

"Miss Gibson?" Field whispered.

"Yep, the old dog's at it again."

"I knew it! He was hanging around near her cabin the other evening, too. A leopard never changes its spots, does it?"

Murray shook his head. "Well, I just thought you should know."

"Yes, thank you for telling me. I'll keep an eye out, and if I catch him anywhere on B Deck, I'll be straight to the chief steward."

7:30am Carrying a glass of orange juice on a small square tray, Field knocked on the cabin door. She waited for her passenger to rise, shuffle into her slippers and unbolt the door, as she had done on every previous morning. But the cabin was as silent as a tomb. The stewardess knocked again, this time a little harder.

"Miss Gibson?"

Receiving no answer, she tried the door handle. To her surprise, it turned, and she stepped inside. The bed sheets were a little more dishevelled than usual and had several small stains, but nothing to warrant any special attention. Gay's evening dress was hanging on the wall by the end of the bed. She knew Gay preferred to place it in the wardrobe herself and left it hanging.

Field's routine was to hang up Gay's yellow dressing gown and leave her black silk pyjamas folded at the foot of the bed with her blue nightgown. Noticing that both the dressing gown and pyjamas were missing, she assumed Gay was wearing them to visit a bathroom. Recalling Camb's comment about her pregnancy, it crossed her mind that she might be suffering a bout of morning sickness. Seeing Gay's only pair of slippers on the floor by the chest of drawers, however, alarmed her. Gay never walked barefoot outside her cabin, and Field instinctively felt something was wrong.

7:50am After returning to cabin 126, Field noticed the untouched orange juice on top of the chest of drawers. She tracked down the bathroom steward, who confirmed that Gay was not in a bathroom. The stewardess was now concerned for the safety of her passenger.

10:20am With temperatures already soaring into the 70s, Frank Hopwood and William Bray were in deck chairs on Promenade Deck. "I wonder why Miss Gibson never appeared for breakfast this morning," a perplexed-looking Hopwood remarked. "It's most unlike her. They say the stewards are unlocking all the empty cabins. I'm starting to really worry."

"Was everything normal last night after I left you at the stairs?" Bray asked.

"Yes. I went into her cabin as usual, put on the light, wished her goodnight and left. It was the same as all the other nights. Apart from one thing: she was probably the most happy she'd been all trip."

"I just don't understand it. Where could she be?"

"I have an awful feeling this is not going to end well."

James Camb approached the two men. Unusually, he was wearing a long-sleeved coat. In the heat of the tropics, most stewards wore short-sleeved shirts during the day and sleeveless ones late at night. He looked suave in his white deck suit, but over-dressed, especially as temperatures would ratchet up by the afternoon. "Good morning, gentleman. Can I get you an ice cream or anything from the pantry?" After some debate, both passengers ordered an ice cream.

As Camb turned and left, a speaker crackled into life. "This is your captain speaking," the voice boomed across the deck. "A first-class lady passenger, Miss Eileen Gibson, cannot be found. Anyone who knows where she is or has any information concerning her, please report at once to the purser. Thank you."

"They cannot find her!" Hopwood exclaimed anxiously. "My God, what's happened!"

Several minutes later, Camb returned with two small bowls of vanilla ice cream. "This is a terrible thing about Miss Gibson," he said.

"Truly dreadful," replied Bray, politely taking his ice cream, although he had now lost his appetite.

"Wouldn't it be funny if she came walking back on deck after all this," Camb remarked.

"I wish to God she would."

On the bridge, the chief steward briefed the captain on the morning's events. Arthur Patey, a reserved, cautious and strict master, reversed the course of the liner, so a sea search could be conducted for the missing passenger, and ordered a full enquiry.

11am Bray and Hopwood were summoned separately to the

bridge, where the chief steward, purser and captain were waiting. As Gay's dining companions, the captain wanted to know whether anything unusual had occurred the night before. They stated that they left Promenade Deck with Gay sometime after half-past midnight and accompanied her to B Deck, with Hopwood escorting her to her cabin. Both men later submitted brief statements typed on the liner's headed notepaper.

During the next hour, Arthur Patey acted like a legal advocate, summoning various people to his office to interrogate them on the matter. The statements enabled the captain to build a picture of what might have happened to the missing passenger. Everything was entered into his log. He next ordered Fred Steer to the bridge.

"You wanted to see me, Captain?" Steer asked nervously.

"Yes. I have reason to believe that you were called to Miss Gibson's cabin last night?"

"That is correct, sir."

"Tell me exactly what happened."

"At about three o'clock last night I was in the first-class pantry when I heard bells ringing. I went up the stairs to the indicator on B Deck and found that both the green and red bulbs were lit. The bells for both the steward and stewardess had been rung, which is unusual, sir. I followed the lights to cabin 126."

"Miss Gibson's cabin?"

"Yes, sir."

"I knocked on the door. There was no response, so I started to open it. When it was open about two inches, a man's voice said, 'It's all right,' and in a split second the door was forced shut. The man was standing with his back to the chest of drawers and slammed the door with his right hand. I returned to the pantry and informed the senior nightwatchman what had happened."

"You told James Murray straightaway?" the chief officer asked.

"Yes, sir."

"Then what?" the captain said.

"We went back to the cabin together. I remained in the portside corridor while he went along the small alleyway to the cabin. After a few minutes he returned, saying everything was quiet."

"Did he try the door?"

"I don't know, sir, you would have to ask him. I then went round the clock."

"Did you see anything suspicious or unusual during your inspection?"

"No, everything was normal."

"Did you recognise the man?"

"It was deck steward Camb, sir."

"Did you actually see his face?"

"The door was slammed shut so quickly I only saw the back of his head and body, but I knew who it was. He was wearing his singlet and blue trousers tied with a brown belt. It was Camb, sir."

The senior officers silently exchanged glances. "But you did not see his face?"

"I knew who it was, sir."

Patey rubbed his brow in thought. "Have you spoken to Camb about this?"

"No, sir."

"You must say that the man you saw in the cabin resembled Camb," Patey wisely instructed, "and you are to tell no one what you saw, especially Camb. Is that understood?"

Steer affirmed it was and left. James Murray was called and confirmed bells were rung around 3am and that he instructed Steer to investigate. When Steer reported back about four minutes later, they returned to the cabin together.

"Then what happened?" enquired the captain.

"I walked down the alleyway and switched off the red and green lights. The cabin door was closed. I was unable to hear any noise or conversation from inside."

"Did you try to enter the cabin?"

"No, sir."

"What did you do?"

"I just listened by the door for about five minutes. I heard nothing."

The captain wondered why he had not been more assertive in his enquiries but, passing over this point, asked, "Was the cabin light on?"

"Yes, there was light coming from the grating above the door."

"What happened after five minutes?"

"I ordered Steer to go round the clock while I reported to the second officer on the bridge."

"What did you report?"

"I informed him that both bells had been rung from cabin 126. I suspected it was accidental because this has happened before at this time of night. He said it was not our place to interfere with passengers' morals. I then returned to cabin 126 – this would have been about 3:20am – and it was in total darkness."

Dismissing Murray, Patey turned to the chief steward. "Let's speak to him now."

11:20am The questioning by the captain was brusque. "Do you know why this first-class passenger is missing, Camb?"

"No, sir."

"You are suspected of being near cabin 126 at 3am last night. Were you?"

Camb paused, panning for nuggets of information from the captain's words, but Patey had played his hand well. There was no suggestion that the deck steward had been positively identified inside the cabin. "No, sir," Camb stated confidently. "I was not near any passenger accommodation after 12:45 this morning, when I retired to bed."

"Noted, but I want you examined by the ship's doctor."

"Why, sir?"

"You are suspected of being involved in the disappearance of Miss Gibson, Camb. It's in your own interests." When there was no response, Patey pressed the point: "Do you agree to a medical examination or not? You may decline but, if you do, I will have to make a note of it in my log."

Grudgingly, Camb agreed. He felt he had little choice. Refusal would be taken as a sign of guilt. He left the bridge, muttering under his breath, "Why all this suspicion? Let's get down to bedrock."

Captain Patey turned to his chief steward. "Was anything heard from the cabin last night?"

"I don't know. That part of the ship is sparsely occupied, but there's someone in the adjoining cabin. An elderly lady, I believe."

"Let's pay her a visit on the way to cabin 126 to see if she can add anything to what we know."

After a discussion with the ship's doctor, Patey concluded that any search for the missing passenger was futile. "It was assumed that Miss Gibson disappeared at some time between 3am and 7:30am today," he wrote in his log, "and that no reasonable hope could be entertained of recovering her by retracing the ship's course any further." The *Durban Castle* resumed her normal heading.

11:50am Henrietta Stephens opened her cabin door to see the captain, the chief steward and the purser standing outside.

"Oh my!" she exclaimed, startled. "Is this about that poor missing girl? I've been told it's the one from the next cabin. Not that we talked much, mind. I didn't even know her name until this morning."

"Yes, Miss Gibson has been reported missing," the captain said gravely. "Mrs Stephens, did you hear anything from her cabin last night?"

She frowned. "Hmm… there was one thing. I was woken in the middle of the night by a clutter. Like someone banging a metal tray. Right outside my cabin, too."

"Can you be more specific?"

"I'm afraid not. It sounded like the crash of a metal tray, that's all. I thought nothing of it."

"Were there any voices?"

Mrs Stephens outstretched a hand to steady herself as the ship gently lolled in the swell. "Not last night, no. The only time I heard voices was when there was a knock on her cabin door and a woman with a deep voice talked to Miss Gibson. Well, it sounded like a woman with a deep voice. I heard noises from her cabin on a few occasions, actually."

"Noises?" asked the chief steward.

"Yes, like she was moving things about. This was late at night, mind."

"And did you see Miss Gibson with anyone?"

"I'm afraid I only saw her once or twice. I've been feeling unwell, so I've been laid up in my cabin for most of the voyage. I do remember one time, though. I think it was the Sunday morning." She paused. "Yes, it was Sunday because I asked her whether she was going to the service. She said she was going to get a book from a steward, but he wasn't there."

"Do you know which steward?"

"No. I must say, this whole affair has quite unsettled my nerves."

"Well, there is no need to be alarmed," the captain said. "You are perfectly safe."

After thanking Mrs Stephens, the three officers stepped inside cabin 126. It looked immaculate, having been tidied and the floor swept. Following instructions from Union Castle headquarters, the porthole was closed and the door padlocked. It was now a crime scene.

12:20pm Back on the bridge, the captain ordered an urgent radio message to be sent to all ships in the vicinity to look out for a female passenger, believed to be lost overboard. Eight minutes later, a brief message was received from the SS *Reventazon*. It was the only response. The cargo ship was covering the route and would make a search of the area. Nothing was found.

*

Members of the Cold Case Jury, as the *Durban Castle* continued its journey, amid growing suspicion and gossip among the crew, Camb wrote to the captain to provide a more detailed explanation of his whereabouts during the night in question. He handed the following note to the chief steward early on Sunday morning.

> *"Durban Castle"*
> *Voyage 35, From Cape Town to Southampton*
> *At Sea, 19 October 1947*

To Captain Patey, Master
Sir,
With reference to my whereabouts at 3am on the 18th, I respectfully beg to state that after locking my deck pantry at approximately 1am, I went forward to the Well Deck where I sat and smoked. I felt myself dozing off to sleep, so I first visited the toilet and then retired. After getting into bed, I carried out my usual practice of smoking one cigarette. My last act was to wind my clock and the time was then a little after 2am. I did not leave the cabin again until we were called at 5.45am.
J. Camb, Deck Steward

His story had changed. He originally told the captain he went to bed at 12:45am, but that was unsustainable. When his cabin mates, such as Bill Pott, turned in at 1am there was no sign of him. The new account was just as unsatisfactory as his first. If Steer was correct, Camb was lying through his teeth, and the captain knew it.

Later on the same morning, Camb was examined by the ship's doctor. Anthony Griffiths found injuries on four areas of the deck steward's body: the left shoulder, the left wrist, the back of his neck and right forearm. The doctor was satisfied that the superficial scratches and abrasions found on the left shoulder and left wrist were old and not inflicted on the night Gay disappeared. He accepted Camb's explanation that they were caused by his scratching in bed due to the humid tropical heat.

There were two injuries possibly caused on the night in question, however. At the back of Camb's neck, on the right, were up to nine one-inch scratches, extremely thin and caused by a sharp object. In the doctor's opinion, they were not caused by fingernails, but "were similar to those inflicted by cat's claws". The injuries to the right wrist were the most probative. With Camb's hand outstretched with palm uppermost, there were up to a dozen scratches, approximately half an inch in length, midway along his forearm. Camb stated they were again self-inflicted by scratching. Griffiths thought "they were suggestive of violence which is unusual, but not unknown, in self-inflicted scratching".

On the advice of Dr Griffiths, Camb sent another note to the captain, explaining in his own words how he sustained the injuries that were found during the medical examination. He wrote:

"Durban Castle"
19 October 1947

Captain Patey, Master
Sir,
At your request, I was fully examined by the surgeon, Dr Griffiths, and he found some slight scratches on my left shoulder and wrist, also a few on my right wrist. These were self-inflicted three or four nights ago while in

bed. I was feeling terribly hot and itchy and I must have scratched myself during my sleep. I remarked during the following morning that I'd "damned well near scratched myself to death", though at the time of writing these marks are healing fast. Also, early last week, I broke a small patch of skin on my neck by a too-vigorous rubbing with a very rough towel. With the friction of the neck-band of my white jackets, this is still a little irritant.

You will receive a full report on today's examination from the surgeon. I am, sir, yours faithfully, James Camb, Deck Steward

The disappearance of Gay Gibson cast a dark shadow over the rest of the journey. Along with a couple of other passengers, William Bray disembarked when the *Durban Castle* made its scheduled stop at the island of Madeira, leaving Frank Hopwood the only one of the three dining companions to arrive at Southampton. Whatever anxieties were gnawing inside him, the deck steward appeared cheerful during the remainder of the voyage. It was to be his last.

On Thursday 24 October, Union Castle informed Southampton Police that it had received a cablegram from the *Durban Castle*. A female passenger had been lost overboard and "there were complications in connection with the disappearance". The police were requested to investigate the matter, and detectives were waiting when the *Durban Castle* arrived back in England.

Chapter 6

REVELATION

Late on Friday 24 October 1947, the *Durban Castle* anchored at Cowes Roads off the Isle of Wight. In the small hours of Saturday morning two police detectives, John Quinlan and Minden Plumley, traversed the short stretch of the Solent from Southampton docks by tug boat and boarded the liner.

Detective Sergeant Quinlan – a burly, monkish-looking man, with thinning hair shaved almost into a tonsure – was a well-respected police officer. Detective Constable Plumley, who had the appearance of a wide boy with his pencil moustache and slicked-back hair, had already gained a reputation for employing questionable methods to secure a confession, and was suspected of pilfering a prisoner's property while in custody. He would resign from the force in less than three months.

After a briefing by the captain and William Turner, an official of the Union Castle Line, the detectives began interviewing passengers and crew. Signed statements were taken from Frank Hopwood, Fred Steer and James Murray. Cabin 126 was opened for a preliminary inspection. By the side of the bed was a large brown suitcase. A small leather attaché case contained several letters of introduction and an army service and pay book. On the chest of drawers was a hairbrush, an alarm clock, a scattering of perfume bottles, a vanity bag and three hardback books. In the alcove by the bed was a copy of *My Life in Art* by the Russian actor and theatre director Konstantin Stanislavski. A blue nightgown was folded neatly on the bed and an elegant evening dress hung forlornly from the wall. These were the ghostly reminders of Gay Gibson.

Five hours after boarding, the detectives were ready to question the first-class deck steward. The following reconstruction picks up the story.

*

5:25am Camb wrung out the mop over the metal bucket and continued cleaning the fore-deck wash house. With little sleep in 24 hours, he felt fatigued and edgy. Aware of footsteps behind him, he turned. Framed in the doorway, like a scene from a movie, were two detectives wearing grey hats and long overcoats.

"James Camb?" Quinlan enquired. The steward nodded. "We are detectives from Southampton CID and we would like to interview you regarding a certain matter. Would you please accompany us to the first-class Smoke Room?"

Camb stuck the mop in the bucket and glanced at the warrant card Quinlan was brandishing. "Can I change out of these first?" he asked, gesturing to his deck uniform. After changing in his cabin, he was accompanied by the police officers to the Smoke Room. Reeking of stale cigarettes, the room was streaked by a faint blue haze from the night before. Seated in armchairs around a circular table near the bar, the gathering looked more like a breakfast business meeting than a police investigation. Standing at the bar, observing proceedings for his Union Castle Line report, was William Turner.

"I have been making enquiries into the disappearance from this ship of a first-class passenger named Miss Gibson," Quinlan began, his voice slow and measured. "I believe you may know something about it."

"Should I know anything about it?" Camb shot back defensively.

"I have reason to believe you can assist me in my enquiry into this matter."

"I know Miss Gibson. I have seen her on the deck and have attended to her, but that's all."

"Have you ever been to Miss Gibson's cabin?"

Camb glanced towards the bar, where Turner was taking notes. "Never."

"Are you sure? It's cabin 126, portside on B Deck."

"I'm sure."

"Is it not a fact that you delivered afternoon tea to Miss Gibson in her cabin?"

Camb was surprised to discover the detectives knew so much detail already. "Yes, but I was stopped from doing so. I only went there once or twice at the beginning of the trip."

"Is it part of your duties to serve tea trays to passengers in their cabins?"

"No, that's the reason I was stopped."

Quinlan paused, looking down at his open notebook. "What time did you finish work on Friday 17 October? That would be the night prior to Miss Gibson's disappearance."

"About one o'clock in the morning."

"Where did you go?"

"I went to the Well Deck for a smoke and was asleep in my bed by 2am."

"Are you sure about that?"

"I was definitely in bed by 2am."

Showing signs of impatience, Constable Plumley cut in. "Would you care to show us your wrists?"

"Sure." Camb removed his coat and rolled up the sleeves of his shirt.

The detectives edged closer to examine his arms. Quinlan noted there were partially healed scratch marks on the inside of his right forearm.

"How do you account for these marks on your wrists?" Plumley asked.

Camb sighed. "Have you ever been in the tropics?"

"No."

"It's hot and humid. You're covered in a film of sweat all day that makes you itch like hell. I nearly scratched myself to death in my sleep during the night."

"Those scratches are not self-inflicted," Plumley retorted. "They're far too serious for that!" Quinlan fired a stern look to his subordinate.

"I've done the same to the inside of my legs."

"Camb, I am not satisfied with your answers. I'm going to make further enquiries and I would like you to accompany me to police headquarters."

The steward paused. "All right, but I would like to get my things."

*

Members of the Cold Case Jury, after escorting James Camb to Southampton Police headquarters, the detectives returned to the liner for a careful examination of the cabin. A palm print was found on the inside of the main door, which was then taken from its hinges and removed. The porthole was opened and forensically examined. Tiny, downy fibres were found clinging to its rim. Several small stains were found on both pillows and bed sheets. These were removed, along with the bed frame and mattress.

The detectives continued to take statements from the crew. At midday they saw Griffiths, the ship's doctor, and impressed upon him that if the marks on the steward's arms were consistent with defensive injuries, he should say so. At the end of the interview,

Griffiths added a handwritten note to the bottom of his original typed report. Separately signed and dated, it read:

The general direction of the abrasions on both wrists was from above downwards and from the inner side towards the outside. They were consistent with injuries that might be inflicted by a person endeavouring to free himself from attempted strangulation from behind.

At just after 5pm, Quinlan and Plumley returned to police headquarters, by which time Camb had been left alone for almost 12 hours. This was a deliberate tactic. Detectives of this era worked on the principle that an innocent person would never confess to something he had not done. Psychological pressure was ratcheted up in the belief the guilty would eventually crack. Leaving a suspect to stew for hours was not the only ploy to induce a suspect to talk. Another was to place Manila folders full of old crime reports on the table to suggest detectives had uncovered more evidence than they had.

By 6:30pm, the interview with James Camb was over an hour old, without much progress for the detectives. This was about to change dramatically.

6:30pm Layers of smoke hung over the cramped interview room like an early morning mist. On one side of the mundane-looking table were Quinlan and Plumley, their notebooks open in front of them. On the other side, lounging in a metal chair, tired and dishevelled, was James Camb, his last cigarette in hand and his crushed packet of Camels lying before him. In no man's land were three empty tea mugs and a glass ashtray full of gnarled cigarette ends.

"I don't want to go all through your movements again," Quinlan said. "Based on our enquiries, I have now established you were in Miss Gibson's cabin that night."

The room fell silent. After thinking for a few moments, Camb looked up. "I want to tell you something. I didn't want to tell you in front of Mr Turner this morning. I had no right to go to her cabin, but I did go down at 11pm that night to ask her if she wanted lemonade with her rum. I saw her in her cabin. She was looking through her luggage for her swimsuit. She said she couldn't find it. She went back upstairs, telling me to leave the rum in the usual place."

"What do you mean by 'leave the rum in the usual place'?"

"The night before Miss Gibson asked me to get her a glass of rum and leave it on the ledge outside the pantry by the Long Gallery."

"Do you remember if she collected her drink on the night of 17 October?"

"Yes, she collected it just before 1am. After that I went to the Well Deck for a smoke before turning in."

"Was Miss Gibson in the habit of being on deck late at night, unaccompanied?"

"Yes. I saw her several times. Once she passed me on deck carrying a clock in her hand."

"Do you know why she was carrying it?"

"No, I don't."

Sensing that the interview was heading nowhere, Quinlan decided to play his trump card. "I think you can tell us more about the disappearance of Miss Gibson than you are saying. I know you were in Miss Gibson's cabin at about three o'clock on the morning of the 18th of October."

"That puts me in a tight spot," Camb muttered, scratching his nose.

"What's that supposed to mean?"

Camb shrugged his shoulders. Exasperated, Quinlan left the interview room, closing the door behind him. A few minutes later, the door was flung open. Quinlan re-entered the room accompanied by Herbert Gibbons, the acting detective inspector. Another chair was dragged to the table. Gibbons, a lean, serious-looking man, sat directly opposite Camb. He pushed the ashtray, mugs and Camel packet to one side, symbolically clearing the decks.

"I have been discussing the situation with Sergeant Quinlan and I understand that up to the present you have denied having been to Miss Gibson's cabin after one o'clock in the morning on the 18th of October. Is this correct?"

"Yes."

"I am sure Sergeant Quinlan has made the position clear to you, and that the implications of a flat denial cannot be lost on you."

Camb frowned. "What do you mean?"

"Let us review the circumstances and see what your position is," Gibbons said pleasantly, sounding more like Camb's lawyer than his interrogator. "If it can be proved conclusively that not only were you in the cabin at 3am, but she was there also, and scientific evidence to show how Miss Gibson disappeared, you must realise the consequences of a flat denial."

Camb was disturbed by the mention of scientific evidence. His hand shaking a little, he leaned over to the ashtray and tapped his cigarette.

"There are also scratch marks on your forearms which have a certain significance," Gibbons continued. "You're being given an opportunity to explain things, but so far you have given a categorical denial that you know anything about the disappearance of Miss Gibson. It will be difficult to give your side of the story if you are called to explain it later."

"Does this mean I murdered her?"

Gibbons hesitated, not knowing what to make of the question.

"Will I be charged with murder?" Camb asked anxiously.

"At this stage I cannot say whether you will be charged with murder or not. You may be able to give a reasonable explanation of the cause of her death, and we will give great consideration to what you say. If you should later decide to make such an explanation, it will be difficult to accept, given your denial now."

Camb's expression changed noticeably. "You mean she might have died in some other way?"

"I am satisfied that you, and you alone, can give an explanation of her death and disappearance," Gibbons stated confidently. "It is for you to decide whether or not you want to provide a statement. I am going to leave you with Sergeant Quinlan. I want to be sure that there is no doubt in your mind of the circumstances in which you are placed." Gibbons nodded at the sergeant and left the room.

Quinlan resumed his questioning. "Are you in the habit of visiting female passengers in their cabins?"

"Well, yes. Some of them like us better than the passengers. I've been with them several times on other trips. Of course, if I was found out, I would have got the sack."

"I understand you have been alleging that Miss Gibson was in a certain condition?"

"She gave me that inference."

"I have reason to believe that this story is untrue."

He shrugged his shoulders. "Well, that's what she told me."

Plumley interjected: "Your answers to Detective Sergeant Quinlan seem to be inconsistent with the true story. It has been established that you were seen in the cabin at 3am."

"What will happen about that then?"

Sensing the interview was rising to its crescendo, Quinlan stated authoritatively, "I believe you have not given us a true account of your movements that night."

Camb fidgeted in his seat. "There might be something in what you say."

"I have no doubt that you were the last person to see Miss Gibson alive."

Revelation

The room sank into a deathly quiet. The detectives looked impassively at the deck steward, who cast his eyes down at the desk. Each minute dragged and seemed like ten. The tension mounted, but still not a word was said. The silence was shattered when Camb scraped his chair across the floor towards the table and stubbed out his cigarette. "Can you take this down in shorthand? I will make a quick statement."

Without showing any emotion, Quinlan nodded, but his pulse quickened. Was this a confession or would Camb merely repeat his story?

"We will take it down just as quickly on the typewriter," Plumley responded. He took a large Imperial typewriter from the table at the back of the room and wound a clean sheet of paper around its platen.

7pm "James Camb," the detective sergeant announced, "you are not obliged to say anything unless you wish to, but anything you say will be written down and may be used in evidence. Do you understand?"

Camb affirmed he did, and to the slow tapping of keys dictated his statement. "I went to Miss Gibson's cabin at about 11 o'clock on Friday 17 October 1947, and during the course of the conversation with her I made an appointment to meet her that night. I knocked at the door after I had finished work at about one o'clock, but there was no answer."

Camb waited for Plumley to catch up, before continuing. "I opened the door of her cabin and found it was empty. I then went forward to the Well Deck, where I sat for about half an hour smoking. I then returned to Miss Gibson's cabin at about two o'clock and found her there."

Camb was changing his story. Quinlan knew the suspect was about to reveal more information, but how much more? He listened, the anticipation rising with every sentence.

"After a short conversation I got into bed, with her consent. Intimacy took place. Whilst in the act of sexual intercourse she clutched at me, foaming at the mouth. I immediately ceased the act, but she was very still. I felt for her heartbeats, but could not find any. She was at that time very still, and I cannot offer any explanation as to how the bells came to be rung, as I most definitely did not touch them myself. Thinking she had fainted, I tried artificial respiration on her. Whilst doing this the nightwatchman knocked at the door and attempted to open it. I shut the door again, saying it was all right.

"Then I panicked, as I thought he had gone to the bridge to report to the officer of the watch, as I did not want to be found in such a compromising position. I bolted the door, and again tried artificial respiration. After a few minutes I could not find a sign of life."

The patter of typewriter keys stopped as Camb hesitated. He did not know whether revealing everything was the correct course of action, but having been up for a straight 24 hours, he only wanted to get this over and sleep. What he said next would shock the world and bring the noose to within an inch of his neck.

"After a struggle with the limp body – by the way, she was still wearing her dressing gown – I managed to lift her to the porthole and pushed her through."

Quinlan was taken aback. This revelation was as good as a murder confession. A jury would think that only a killer desperate to hide his tracks would dispose of a body in such a callous way. The thought of promotion even flashed through his mind.

Plumley was typing furiously as Camb added: "I am fairly certain at the time she was dead, but I was terribly frightened. I then went forward and turned in. The time would be about 3:30am."

"Is that all?" Quinlan asked. Camb nodded. The sheet of paper was pulled from the typewriter and presented to the steward to sign.

After reading it, Camb threw the sheet of foolscap back at the detective. "This is full of typos," he said in disgust. The constable was quietly livid at being shown up in front of his superior. Quinlan ordered the statement to be retyped.

After Camb signed it, Quinlan asked: "Anything else you want to change or add?"

"No, I'm glad to get it off my mind."

As Quinlan stood up to leave, Camb asked anxiously, "What's going to happen about this? My wife must not know. If she does, I will do away with myself."

Quinlan ignored the last remark. With this statement, he believed the state would do the job for him.

*

Members of the Cold Case Jury, Herbert Gibbons advised Camb that it was in his interest to give his side of the story, but this was not the case. If he admitted he was in the cabin that night he would also have to explain how Gay's body was missing. He would have to confess that he pushed the body through the porthole. And anyone hearing *that* would rightly be suspicious that he had committed murder.

The police had no forensic evidence to place Camb in cabin 126 at the time Gay disappeared. They had evidence that he had been in the cabin – the palm print on the inside of the cabin door was later positively matched to Camb's left hand – but this was of little value, since he belatedly admitted to being in Gay's cabin earlier on the Friday evening. The only evidence that placed him in the cabin at the critical time was the testimony of Fred Steer, who never saw the man's face. If Camb had continued to deny it was him, insisting that the nightwatchman was mistaken, it would have been one word against another, with Camb holding the get-out-of-jail-free card of presumed innocence.

When confronted by Gibbons during the interview, Camb

shifted his position from outright denial to an admission that Gay had died naturally in his arms. Fearing the police had a watertight case placing him in the cabin at the critical time, Camb possibly believed that his best defence was no longer to deny being there but simply to deny killing her. At his trial, the prosecution claimed that the police had well-nigh invited him to invent something, and he had obliged by dreaming up the natural-death story. But is it not equally plausible that he realised disposing of the body had failed to put him in the clear, and it was now time to simply tell the truth? Whichever account is correct, from this point onwards Camb never deviated from his statement, only adding further details when asked at his trial.

Before giving his statement, Camb asked, "Does this mean I murdered her?" – a strange question from someone who allegedly had his hands around the neck of his victim. Was he bluffing or trying to reconcile what had happened in the cabin with the view of the police? After his statement, his concern was to keep the knowledge of his atrocious behaviour from his wife. Is this reaction more typical of an apprehended philanderer than a murderer?

On Sunday 26 October, James Camb was charged with the murder of Gay Gibson. Looking shocked, he reportedly exclaimed, "My God, I did not think it would be as serious as this." Within hours, a Sunday paper disclosed that police suspected he strangled the actress before disposing of her body through the porthole. The source could only have been a detective on the case. Suspicion fell on Plumley, an allegation he later denied in court {see *Exhibit 8*}.

Later that day a message was circulated internationally. It read:

A woman passenger, Miss Eileen Gibson, aged 21 years, went overboard approximately 250 miles west of Cape Verde. Information of a body being recovered from the sea or washed up on shores approximating this area to be notified to the Chief Constable, Southampton, England, remains to be carefully preserved. Gibson described as: 5'5", well-built, full round face, eyes brown, pointed chin, left eyebrow slightly higher than right, good even teeth, full lips, auburn hair, short nails, takes size 4 shoes. Last known to be dressed in lady's black pyjamas, believed poplin material, and lightweight yellow flowered kimono. A man has been charged with the murder of this woman.

No trace was ever found.

The wheels of British justice began to turn rapidly. The police investigation had only just begun, and soon more was discovered about the deck steward. The defence team was also making enquiries, especially about Gay's health. After appearing at Southampton Magistrates' Court, Camb was remanded in custody. In November, the committal hearing began. This would determine whether there was enough evidence to place the case before a jury. In effect, it was a dress rehearsal for the trial. It concluded that James Camb was to stand trial for the murder of Gay Gibson at the next Hampshire Assizes. However, on 2 December 1947, the defence counsel applied for an adjournment to allow witnesses to travel from South Africa. It was granted.

The delay would change the ultimate outcome of the case.

Chapter 7

COURTROOM DUELS

Less than four months after the committal hearing, James Camb stood trial for his life at the Great Hall of Winchester Castle. The medieval hall, with its vaulted roof, stained-glass windows and compound columns, was an imposing cathedral of justice, a fitting venue for one of the most dramatic British murder trials of the 20th Century. Its most famous artefact, King Arthur's Round Table hanging on the flint wall above the judge's bench, only added to the historic atmosphere. Its iconic presence had loomed over proceedings when the sea-going adventurer and pirate Sir Walter Raleigh was tried for treason here in 1603.

The wooden court was traditionally arranged. Tables and benches formed an open square with a space in front of the judge – the well. Prominently displayed on a raised platform in the well were items from cabin 126: the white-enamelled metal bed, the door, the bell-pushes and the porthole. Ironically, it looked like a set from an Agatha Christie play. It needed only a red curtain and Gay Gibson to enter at the denouement to reveal what really happened on the *Durban Castle*. As in life, there was theatre to her death.

The trial was a series of intertwining duels, the outcome of which would determine whether a man walked free or stepped onto the gallows. Not only was the evidence contested, there was a clash of legal minds – Joshua Casswell for the defence and Geoffrey Roberts for the prosecution. Only three weeks before, the adversaries had duelled over the life of Ann Cornock in "The Body in the Bath" trial. The case against the defendant was so strong a guilty verdict appeared inevitable. Mrs Cornock claimed she found her husband dead in the bath and, after having a cup of tea with a male friend, telephoned the police three hours later. The husband's bruised body with ligature marks on his wrists and ankles told a different story. Yet, against all the odds, Casswell managed to secure an acquittal from the jury. The two legal gladiators now faced each other again in the historic arena of the Great Hall, with Roberts prosecuting another case in which a guilty verdict seemed to be in the palm of his hand. Another defeat was unthinkable.

The two men were very different. Geoffrey "Khaki" Roberts was an imposing and forceful man. At six feet three inches and weighing nearly 19 stone, it is little wonder he had played rugby for England. The experienced prosecutor was part of the legal team at Nuremburg, where leading Nazis were tried after the war. Casswell was an amateur actor with a resonant voice, ideal qualities in a barrister, and regularly took the murder briefs of those unable to afford legal counsel. He later recalled that before the death penalty was abolished in the United Kingdom, there was an electric tension that fizzed throughout a murder trial. The shadow of the noose hung over the prisoner in the dock, and the responsibility for life and death fell on the shoulders of the legal advocates. Although the days of a public hanging were long gone, crowds still gathered to watch the duel for life inside the courtroom.

By early on Thursday 18 March 1948, a long queue had formed outside the Great Hall, far too many to be accommodated in the packed courtroom. Despite waiting for hours, those who were admitted were seated in an area to the right of the judge with an obscured view, although none appeared disappointed. The press box could not hold the throng of reporters who had flocked to cover the case. Thirty were seated below the dock and behind the counsels' benches. There was only one empty seat. Camb's wife, Margaret, refused to attend the four-day trial.

The conversation echoing around the draughty hall was silenced instantly when James Camb, accompanied by three prison officers, stepped into the prisoner's dock. Smartly dressed in a double-breasted navy suit, with meticulously groomed black hair, he exuded debonair confidence. He stood waiting for the arrival of the man who would pronounce his fate.

At precisely 10am, everyone stood as Mr Justice Malcolm Hilbery, characteristically draped in ermine and a flowing wig, took his place on a throne-like seat that rose imperiously above the court. The slightest of nods to cue the court to sit was followed by an almost dismissive wave of his right hand to commence proceedings. The clerk of the assize rose and faced the dock. "James Camb, you stand charged upon the indictment of murder, and the particulars state that, on 18 October last year, on the high seas, you did murder Eileen Gibson. To that charge do you plead guilty or not guilty?"

His response was firm and calm. "Not guilty." The drama, and the fight for his life, had begun.

The following narrative highlights the most important exchanges of the trial. It is not chronological or a complete summary – this is provided in the trial minutes {see *Exhibit 8*}.

Delivered by Roberts, the opening speech for the prosecution was impressive. He stressed that Camb knew what had happened to Gay Gibson but lied repeatedly about his involvement in her death. Either Camb throttled the actress and pushed her lifeless body through the porthole to destroy the deadly evidence against him, or she was rendered unconscious and killed when she was thrown into the ocean. Looking directly at the jury with outstretched hands, Roberts said:

"The prisoner has put forward a defence that she died a natural death in his arms. Can you possibly accept that? Is there not one fact conclusive against it? The fact is the prisoner disposed of the body. If she had died naturally in his arms, what would have been easier for him than to have slipped unobserved from the cabin? The next morning this girl would have been found in her bed, having died a natural death, a fact a doctor could have established in two minutes. Can you imagine the prisoner, if this was the manner of death, going through the considerable effort to lift the lifeless body up and then push her through the porthole?"

Roberts wanted to convince the jury that the defendant's behaviour was compelling circumstantial evidence of his guilt. By contrast, if the defence could show that Gay might have welcomed the attentions of the steward and the medical evidence was consistent with a natural death, there could be sufficient doubt to secure an acquittal. And so the battle lines were drawn.

If James Camb was on trial for his life, Gay Gibson was on trial after death. Her character, conduct and health were subjected to intense scrutiny. Two very different pictures were delineated by the prosecution and the defence. This duel began at the end of the second day of the trial when the prosecution called Ellen "Daisy" Gibson. The following are abridged exchanges between Roberts and Mrs Gibson.

Counsel: You are the mother of Eileen Gibson?

Gibson: Yes. I am very proud to be the mother of Eileen Gibson.

Counsel: Generally speaking, for the whole of her life, how was her health?

Gibson: Excellent. She was one of the finest types of English womanhood – physically, mentally and morally.

It was obvious from the first exchanges that Daisy was not going to accept that her daughter had any flaws. After establishing details of their time in South Africa, Roberts focused on Gay's health, knowing the defence was to make it an issue.

Counsel: You never had any trouble with her on account of her health?

Gibson: Only her right ear; she had an infection there.

Counsel: During your time in South Africa did you see any traces of ill-health in her?

Gibson: None whatever. Her health was excellent.

Counsel: When you last saw your daughter, was she a healthy woman?

Gibson: Yes, perfect.

The questions for the prosecution were short and effective. The defence had an unenviable task. Without losing the sympathy of the jury, Casswell needed to show that the grieving mother was wrong about her only daughter, preparing the ground for the defence witnesses who would testify later. He began softly, establishing points about her daughter that would cause no offence, before taking aim at the contentions that Gay had perfect health and no romantic attachments.

Counsel: In December 1946, did you hear that she had been taken ill?

Gibson: Never.

Counsel: Did you hear of her having an illness in July 1946?

Gibson: No, I was in Persia then. She had a septic hand when she came back from Germany. It was burnt with an electric iron and for a time she was acting with her hand in a bandage.

Recall that in June 1946, Gay was involved with the army driver Pierre in Germany. Was the burn on her hand actually a result of their cigarette burning ritual? If so, it appears Daisy had been fed a story by her daughter. Determined that her daughter's reputation would not be traduced, her clipped answers reflected a growing resentment for the intrusive questions. Casswell focused next on Gay's time in South Africa.

Counsel: Did you know she was drinking heavily, among other things, vodka?

Gibson: No, she would not drink vodka.

Counsel: Did she suddenly decide not to go on acting in *Golden Boy*, but to return to England?

Gibson: She said she could not stand the attitude of her associates in the play. It was not an excuse; she was thoroughly disgusted with them.

Counsel: But she suddenly decided to return to England?

Gibson: Yes, she had been dying to get back to England. She did not decide it suddenly. She had an opportunity to return, and took it.

Counsel: What was the opportunity?

Gibson: She had an introduction to the management at the Abbey Theatre in Dublin.

The prosecution fished out five letters of introduction the police had discovered among Gay's possessions in her cabin. One was for the Abbey Theatre, Dublin, two for theatres in London and two for dramatic agents. Even if she was returning to England for other reasons, it seems clear she wanted to resume her acting career. All the letters were written after she was released from the cast of *Golden Boy*; one was dated the day before she flew to Cape Town. The rush suggests her departure to England was not planned well in advance.

Counsel: Did you approve of her receiving £500 from a man she had only known a short time?

Gibson: It was a business proposition. Charles Schwentafsky was ready to back her in a career as a business proposition.

Counsel: Did you know your daughter was going about with several men in Johannesburg?

Gibson: My daughter was not going about with men. She was not interested in men. Her career was her life.

Counsel: Did she ever tell you that she had a contraceptive device?

Gibson: No. She told me practically everything. She told me everything.

Counsel: Did you know that she consulted Dr Schoub for advice?

Gibson: I am sure she never did. My daughter would consult me if she wished for advice. She had a poor opinion of Dr Schoub.

Counsel: Did you know that she consulted Dr Schoub on the ground of pregnancy?

Gibson: My daughter was not pregnant.

Counsel: Do you know she was telling everybody she was pregnant?

Gibson: No. My daughter and I were very close friends. We never had any secrets from each other.

Despite her cast-iron certainty, Daisy knew less about her daughter than she thought, or was not prepared to divulge more. This was confirmed when Detective Sergeant Quinlan took the witness stand. He stated that an unused diaphragm and a tube of contraceptive jelly were found in Gay's suitcase, forcing the judge to use his gavel for the first and only time to quell the clamour echoing around the hallowed walls of the Great Hall. Only in an English courtroom is it possible to accuse a man of strangling a young woman and pushing her body through a porthole, only to have the greatest consternation provoked by a contraceptive in a suitcase.

It did raise questions, though. Despite efforts by the prosecution to portray Gay as an innocent young girl, the contraceptive unquestionably confirmed other evidence that Gay was sexually active. As Gay and her latest crush, Charles Schwentafsky, were likely to be apart for some considerable length of time, if not permanently, it suggested something else: Gay was open to the idea of sexual activity with someone else. And if this were accepted, why would she not be open to having sex with a good-looking steward during a voyage?

The duel resumed when the defence called the three witnesses who had travelled from South Africa. Mike Abel testified that Gay had fainted in his presence on three occasions and told him she was pregnant. Abel's cross-examination by Roberts was uncomfortable. Reluctantly, he admitted that the expenses for his trip to England were being met in full. "It's a nice little trip for you, is it not?" Roberts goaded. Abel took the bait, but ended up agreeing with the barrister. The whole tenor of the questioning was that Abel was biased, providing the answers the defence wanted to hear in exchange for a paid trip to England. The evidence of the South African witnesses became tainted by the insinuation of perjury-for-a-holiday.

Abel was a well-chosen target. Roberts did not adopt the same line of questioning with Dr Ena Schoub, Gay's confidante in South Africa. She had been reluctant to undertake the seven-week round trip, only agreeing to testify when it was impressed upon her that a man's life was at stake. Her testimony was confident, credible and reasonable. It is surprising that Casswell did not fully utilise this witness to recover some of the moral high ground lost to the prosecution during Abel's brutal cross examination.

The doctor was the best of the witnesses from Africa. Gay had informed her that she had asthma and had been told it would be better for her to be in Johannesburg after suffering many asthmatic attacks in Durban. By mid-August, Gay had also confided that her period was two weeks late. Henry Gilbert testified that after rehearsals one night, Gay fainted in the middle of a busy street. She was picked up and placed into a car of another cast member to recover. Although there was no decisive victory for the defence on the issue of Gay's character and known health problems, it had made its point. Gay was not in perfect health.

The next duel was over the physical and medical evidence. Dr Donald Teare, a 36-year-old pathologist and lecturer in forensics, was called by the prosecution. Roberts quickly established that Camb had sufficient time to strangle his victim.

Counsel: If the throat is firmly clasped between the fingers, how long a period would elapse before unconsciousness?

Teare: A matter of seconds, probably not more than 15.

Counsel: And how soon, if the same pressure was maintained, would the victim die from suffocation?

Teare: Probably within a minute.

Teare also confirmed that blood-flecked frothing at the mouth was consistent with strangulation. During his cross-examination, Casswell opened by asking questions on an issue that surprised both the prosecution and the witness.

Counsel: Did you know that a sample from one of the sheets taken away from the cabin showed quite a lot of dried urine?

Teare: No, I did not.

A urine stain on the top bed sheet was missed by the police scientists, but had been found by Dr Frederick Hocking, a pathologist and Fellow of the Royal Institute of Chemists, in his examination of the physical evidence for the defence. A flurry of shuffling papers and anxious-looking faces on the prosecution table showed they were unaware of the evidence. Casswell pushed ahead.

Counsel: It is very likely to be the last act of a person before death?

Teare: Yes.

This statement produced palpable relief in the courtroom, a measure of comfort drawn from knowing that Gay Gibson had most likely died in her cabin. It removed the most chilling narrative from the arsenal of the prosecution: that Gay had been merely unconscious when she was pushed into shark-infested waters.

Having elicited from the pathologist that the passing of urine was likely whether a person died from strangulation or natural causes, Casswell believed it was safe to continue with his line of questioning. He was wrong. The grenade he had thrown into the court now exploded.

Counsel: If a person suffering from asthma and some kind of heart disease passes out during sexual intercourse, I suggest that is equally consistent with the evidence found on the bed as with the theory of strangulation?

Teare: No, I would not agree. In my experience, death from asphyxia, which includes strangulation, is frequently associated with terminal urination.

Counsel: I suggest that death from asphyxia without strangulation will lead equally to the same result?

Teare: It may, but you ask me if equally, and I say the chances are not equal.

The prosecution exploited the gift of the new evidence. Like a matador's estocada, Roberts drove the point home with deadly intent during his re-examination of the medical expert.

Counsel: Now you know the defence have ascertained the presence of urine on the bed sheets, does that strengthen your view as to whether the death in this case was from strangulation?

Teare: It does, considerably.

Little wonder, then, the prosecution felt the admission of the urine-stained sheet had been an own goal by the defence. Indeed, Roberts was at a loss as to understand why Casswell introduced the evidence. If it was Casswell's intention to show that Gay died in the cabin, as Camb claimed, it was the most pyrrhic of victories.

Dr Hocking was the first of two medical experts to be called by the defence. His analysis of the urine on the sheets showed there was no blood present. Casswell pressed home its significance:

Counsel: Is there anything in this case which, in your view, indicates rape or attempted rape?

Hocking: Nothing.

If Casswell thought he had scored an important point for the defence, this was quickly negated by a rapier-like interposition from the bench.

Judge: Is there anything which suggests there was sexual intercourse?

Hocking: No.

Roberts was to later admit the prosecution failed to exploit the obvious significance of this point for their case.

Despite the lack of a body, physical evidence was left in the cabin. Of particular interest were several small bloodstains on the top and bottom bed sheets, an analysis of which showed the blood did not come from Camb. According to Hocking, the bloodstains were actually smears containing cells from the lining of the mouth and constituents of saliva. He stated that bloodied saliva was less likely with strangulation than some other causes, such as incipient heart failure. He conceded, however, that both strangulation and natural death were consistent with the medical evidence.

Professor James Webster, a 50-year-old Scot with a noticeable squint in one eye, was the director of the forensic laboratory at Birmingham. He contradicted Donald Teare when he took to the witness stand. He gave four possible causes of natural death consistent with the evidence: the bursting of a brain aneurism; heart failure from cardiac disease; asthmatic heart failure; and heart failure brought about by a "septic focus", such as Gay's chronic ear infection. He claimed that the bursting of a brain aneurism would result in terminal urination and the forensic evidence pointed to death from natural causes as more likely than strangulation. Roberts was keen to neutralise this evidence.

Counsel: You have given four possible causes of natural death?

Webster: Yes.

Counsel: Which one are you saying is as likely as strangulation? Or are you saying that the possibility of the four added together amount to the same probability as strangulation?

Webster: Not added together, but individually.

Having received this answer, Roberts quickly moved on and Casswell failed to return to this crucial point when he re-examined Webster. It was a mistake. Webster appears to be saying that, in his opinion, any of the four natural causes were as likely as strangulation.

This would imply that, in terms of odds, it was four to one against strangulation, based on the medical evidence alone. Despite his propensity to interpose, the judge was conspicuously silent and Webster was never asked to develop his view.

Without a body, a pathologist has no firm foundation on which to build his scientific opinion. The inordinate mass of tangled possibilities and unknowns makes it virtually impossible to disprove any claims about cause of death. It is hardly surprising, then, that the medical evidence regarding the cause of death in this case was protracted, detailed and contradictory. Taken as a whole, it showed only that the physical evidence was consistent with both strangulation and natural causes; the defence and prosecution had cancelled each other out. Indeed, Travers Humphreys, a senior judge at the time, commented that this case was highly unusual in that "the medical expert evidence called on both sides left open the answer to the question, usually a matter of common ground: was any murder proved to have been committed?"

The medical experts also focused on the injuries to Camb's right forearm, which were initially examined by the ship's doctor, Dr Griffiths, on the *Durban Castle* the day after Gay was reported missing. The injuries were photographed by the police a week later when the liner docked at Southampton. Based on the photographic evidence, Hocking testified that some of the marks appeared "far too deep" to be scratches and were consistent with a convulsive gripping, digging into the flesh, at the moment of death or at the end of sexual intercourse.

Webster provided the greatest insight regarding the marks. He stated those on Camb were atypical of strangulation; they were far too high up the forearm, without any scratches on the thumb and back of the hand where Gay would have clawed at Camb's grip, trying to pry it loose. Teare agreed that it was more usual to see marks on the wrists or ball of the thumb, "but I do not see these are so very much above the wrist". The key point, however, appears to be not the position of the scratches on the forearm, but the absence of marks on the back of the hands and thumb, suggesting strangulation was a little less likely.

The judge asked Webster to view the photograph of Camb's forearm, reminding him that Griffiths had counted nine to 12 marks:

Judge: Is it six or seven we can see in the photograph?

Webster: Seven.

Judge: So we have two to five more to account for. Would you, from the evidence you have heard, suppose they were nearer the thumb.

Webster: I do not know, my lord.

Judge: But if that were so, would that indicate the possibility of strangulation?

Webster: As I have said, my lord, I cannot exclude the possibility.

Clearly, Mr Justice Hilbery was on a fishing expedition for the prosecution at this point. In his questioning of Griffiths, Roberts had failed to establish the position of all the marks, probably unaware of the importance Dr Hocking and Professor Webster would attach to it, yet it was hardly for the judge to invite Webster to suppose where they might have been located. If there had been marks "nearer the thumb" they could only have been superficial wounds, because they were no longer visible when the photograph was taken.

This case was not decided by the medical experts, however, but by the circumstantial evidence. The most important of which is likely to be a question that has been in your mind, no doubt, for some time. If he was innocent, what motivated Camb to push Gay's body through the porthole? This could only be answered by the man himself. When James Camb took to the witness stand, the tense, life-and-death duel reached its climax.

Chapter 8

HANGING IN THE BALANCE

The prosecution rested its case towards the end of the second day of the trial. In his opening speech for the defence, Joshua Casswell reminded the jury that his client was not to be judged on his actions in disposing of the dead body, but whether he murdered Gay Gibson. After the cabin door was pushed ajar by the nightwatchman, Camb's anxiety turned to sheer panic:

"He ought to have gone to the doctor straightaway; he ought to have communicated with somebody; he ought to have seen to it that other assistance was brought to this girl; but in moments like that sometimes human nature asserts itself and the first thing one thinks of in a panic is self. He knew that if he should be found in that cabin it was the end of his employment… it would inevitably mean that he would be instantly dismissed and he would never get any similar job with any reputable line again."

After a relatively brief speech outlining the defence case, Casswell sat down, and Mr Molony, the second defence counsel, called James Camb to the witness box. Patiently, Molony guided the defendant to recall the events leading up to midnight on 18 October. Eventually, questioning turned to the events immediately preceding the fateful encounter in cabin 126.

Counsel: After you tidied up, where did you go?

Camb: I locked the Deck Pantry and went to cabin 126. It would be a few minutes after 1am.

Counsel: Was there any light in the cabin?

Camb: Yes. I knocked on the door, opened it, but there was no one there. I then went to the crew Well Deck, where I stayed for a full hour.

Counsel: Where did you go then?

Camb: I went back to cabin 126.

Counsel: Did you go into the cabin?

Camb: I did.

The question of how he was greeted was carefully sidestepped. Camb stated that Gay was wearing a yellow dressing gown and the only illumination was from the cylindrical light next to the bed.

Counsel: After you entered the cabin, what happened next?

Camb: Miss Gibson reclined on the bed, and I sat on the edge of the bed.

Counsel: You could see she was wearing a quilted dressing gown. What other garments did she have on?

Camb: At that time I had no idea, but later I saw she was wearing nothing at all.

Counsel: Was there any conversation?

Camb: We talked about the dullness of the dance.

Counsel: And what happened after about 10 minutes?

Camb: I climbed onto the bed beside her.

Counsel: How did you see she had no clothing underneath her dressing gown?

Camb: When she unzipped her dressing gown, which fastened up the front, full length.

Counsel: What happened after that?

Camb: There was a certain amount of preliminary love-play and then sexual intercourse took place.

The next questions elicited the details. According to Camb, they adopted the missionary position, with Gay's head resting in the crook of his left arm and his right arm resting on her hip. Gay's right hand was around his neck and her left hand holding his right arm.

Counsel: What happened in the end?

Camb: Just as intercourse would normally have come to an end she suddenly heaved under me as though she were gasping for breath, as though she was taking a deep breath.

Counsel: What happened to her body?

Camb: It stiffened for a fraction of a second and then relaxed, completely limp.

Counsel: Did you notice anything about her hands?

Camb: Her right arm was still around my neck when she heaved against me. That arm automatically tightened. The left arm, holding my right forearm, gripped tightly. All this happened in a matter of seconds.

Counsel: Did you feel anything in your right forearm at the time her grip tightened?

Camb: No.

The defence counsel was inviting his client to state that Gay Gibson inflicted the wounds on his arms in her death throes, but Camb was rigidly sticking to his police statement. He did not want to be accused of telling any more lies.

Counsel: What did you do when her body showed these symptoms?

Camb: I immediately got off the bed. She was completely relaxed as though in a dead faint. One eye was just slightly open. Her mouth was a little open, too. There was a faint line of bubbles, which I assumed to be froth, just on the edge of her lips. It was a muddy colour, and appeared to be blood-flecked.

Counsel: What was your reaction?

Camb: I was rather stunned for the moment.

He stood by the bed trying to revive her by massaging her chest and applying artificial respiration for 20 minutes. Counsel then referenced the bells that brought the nightwatchman to the cabin.

Counsel: We have heard that two bells were rung for cabin 126. Did you know anything about that at the time?

Camb: No.

Counsel: How did you know the nightwatchman had been summoned?

Camb: There was a very light tap on the door and it immediately opened.

Counsel: Where were you?

Camb: Standing by the bed.

Counsel: After he opened the door, did you push it in his face?

Camb: Not quite as literally as that, but I did shut the door to prevent him entering.

Counsel: Did you think that the man at the door had recognised you?

Camb: I doubted it at the time.

Counsel: Did you think a report would be made by him?

Camb: Yes, immediately.

Counsel: When you realised this, what was your sensation?

Camb: One of complete panic, I'm afraid.

Counsel: What were you afraid of?

Camb: Being found in that cabin. I knew that in the circumstances of being found in a female passenger's cabin I should lose my job and forfeit any chance of employment in any shipping company for that matter.

According to his testimony, Camb continued to revive Gay for a further 15 minutes but was convinced she was dead. This led to the questions on which the entire case would pivot.

Counsel: What did you decide to do?

Camb: I confess now it sounds very foolish, but I hoped to give the impression that she had fallen overboard and deny all knowledge of having been to that cabin, in the hope that the captain's inquiries would not be too severe.

Counsel: What were you going to do then?

Camb: Dispose of her body by pushing it through the porthole.

Counsel: What did you actually do?

Camb: I lifted her up and pushed her through.

The questions and answers were so matter-of-fact, any sympathy the jury might have had for the defendant quickly evaporated. The jury might have also been left with the impression that pushing a body through a porthole was an easy task. It was no such thing. During an adjournment, 18-year-old Peggy Durrant, a petite court official, was pushed through the porthole exhibit by several police officers as a light-hearted prank. The porthole was an exact replica – 16¾" in diameter and the same height from the floor as in cabin 126 (although Camb was aided by the bed, which was situated below the porthole). Even working together, they struggled to lift and squeeze her through the tiny aperture. To this day, Peggy does not know how Camb managed his grisly task.

The examination continued on the third day, covering subsequent events, including the police questioning. The defence elicited explicit statements from Camb that he had not killed or harmed Gay Gibson. The cross-examination was conducted by the fearsome Roberts. He rose and glanced at the jury before staring at the defendant. The first salvo of questioning began.

Counsel: Would you describe yourself as a truthful man?

Camb: I think so.

Counsel: You do. You were the last person to see Miss Gibson alive?

Camb: Yes.

Counsel: You put her through the porthole at 3am on the morning of 18 October?

Camb: Yes.

Counsel: Did you for the next eight days make untrue statements regarding this?

Camb: I did, yes.

Counsel: When did you decide to alter your story?

Camb: In the police headquarters.

Counsel: Why?

Camb: I realised by then that I was definitely incriminated by Steer.

Counsel: Did you realise it was no good in persisting with that particular story?

Camb: I proceeded to tell the truth.

Counsel: You told an untrue story until you felt that it would not serve its purpose of saving you?

Camb: Yes.

Counsel: Don't you call that curious conduct for a truthful person?

Camb: I should say it was beastly conduct.

Roberts knew all too well that juries rarely give the benefit of doubt to liars. In less than five minutes, the case was looking difficult for the defence. The next salvo made matters worse.

Counsel: You realise that the body of a dead person is the most valuable evidence as to the cause of death?

Camb: Yes.

Counsel: If the second story, the one you are telling now, is true, you destroyed the best evidence in your favour, did you not?

Camb: I did not think of that at the time.

Counsel: Please apply yourself to it now and answer the question.

Camb: I did, yes.

Counsel: If your second story is as false as your first, you destroyed the most deadly evidence against you, did you not?

Camb: Yes.

Robert's questioning was masterly, and undoubtedly had a major impact on the jury, but it was specious. If his story was true, Camb did not see Gay's body as proof that she had died naturally but as a problem that would end his career at sea. A narcissist, his "curious instinct" considered only his needs and nothing else. However, with his next onslaught, Roberts honed his argument.

Counsel: According to your second story, this girl died in your arms a natural death?

Camb: Yes.

Counsel: Why in the world could you not slip out of the cabin leaving her there?

Camb: I did not think of it.

Counsel: Is that not the first thing anyone would think of, if you were satisfied she was dead?

Camb: I could not say. At that moment, I was not thinking clearly at all.

And Camb was not thinking clearly in the witness box. He had previously stated that he was stunned, tried to revive her, but when the nightwatchman arrived, panicked. But if he thought he had not been identified, why did he not leave when he thought the coast was clear? The judge asked him just this.

Judge: You were quite satisfied that you had not been identified as the man in the cabin?

Camb: Yes, I thought so at the time.

Judge: So what necessity was there to do anything but slip out of the cabin?

Camb: My intention was to give the impression she had disappeared of her own accord.

Judge: If she was found dead in her cabin, nobody could know if anyone had been in there.

Camb: Enquiries might have been made and I might have been incriminated.

Judge: How could you have been incriminated if you were not identified by the nightwatchman?

Camb: At that time the description was of a "dark person". There were few dark persons on the ship at that time. I was sure to be interrogated by the captain among the dark persons on board.

The last answer makes no sense at all. When Camb shut the

cabin door he could not know the details of the description that might be provided. Presumably, he thought the nightwatchman had seen the colour of his hair. Indeed, Steer had told the captain the man he saw had black hair, but this was hours later. Camb was improvising with hindsight. He knew very well he would be interrogated by the captain because he had a reputation of liaisons with female passengers, some of them unwelcome. Of course, this is not something he would want to state in his defence. Imprisoned by his lies and reputation, Camb was pulling the noose around his neck with each answer.

Roberts turned his attention to the most damning evidence, the ringing of the bells.

Counsel: Why did the nightwatchman come to the door?

Camb: I have no idea.

Counsel: Who rang those two bells?

Camb: I don't know.

Counsel: What would you expect a passenger to do who, in the night, objected to the advances of a member of the crew?

Camb: Shout.

Counsel: Not much good shouting. Is not ringing the bells much better?

Camb: They both amount to the same thing.

Counsel: That is what she did, is it not?

Camb: She did not touch the bell.

Counsel: Who did then?

Camb: I don't know.

Counsel: Did you have to work quickly to silence her before the bell was answered?

Camb: No.

An engineer had previously testified that the bell system was working correctly. Therefore, someone must have pushed the bells, even accidentally. Roberts was not finished.

Counsel: In your association with Miss Gibson in her cabin that night, you received no injuries from her at all?

Camb: To the best of my knowledge, no.

Counsel: You are not suggesting some of them were caused by Miss Gibson?

Camb: Some of them might have been. What I said was that I had caused the original scratches.

Counsel: This is what you said in your statement: "I received no injury of any sort while in the company of Miss Gibson". Do you want to alter that now?

Camb: No.

If Gay inflicted the scratch wounds to his forearm, as he would later claim after his trial, Camb clearly lied in his police statement. He was now so entangled by the web of lies he had already spun there was no escape when faced by his nemesis. Roberts moved on, but there was no respite from the inquisition.

Counsel: You say Miss Gibson was not wearing her pyjamas.

Camb: No.

Counsel: What has happened to the black pyjamas?

Camb: I have not the slightest idea.

Counsel: Miss Field says they were in the cabin the previous day but were missing the next morning. Why were the pyjamas and the dressing gown both missing?

Camb: I did not know she had any black pyjamas.

Counsel: If you did not know she had black pyjamas and she was wearing them, this shows you did not access her body, does it not?

Camb: She was not wearing any pyjamas.

Counsel: I suggest your story is wholly untrue. The pyjamas were missing in the same way as the dressing gown. I suggest your second story is just as untrue as the first.

Camb: No.

When Eileen Field entered the empty cabin at 7:30am, just four hours after Gay died, she noticed that the actress's slippers were on the floor and her blue nightgown was folded at the foot of the bed, but her yellow dressing gown and black pyjamas were missing. Where were the black pyjamas? If Camb was telling the truth, the black pyjamas should have been in Gay's cabin.

To the delight of the press, the absence of Gay's black pyjamas was a memorable feature of the case. The 'Mystery of Gay Gibson's Black Pyjamas' was the *News of the World* headline. This was fuelled by a salacious rumour that the pyjamas were in the cabin of a distinguished passenger who had promised to produce the missing garments if the steward was found guilty. If this was true, and the passenger had come forward, it would have shown Camb was telling the truth about this aspect of the case, giving greater credibility to the whole of his account.

Was Gay really naked underneath her dressing gown? Or, in wanting to give the impression that she was anticipating sex, did Camb make a big mistake by inventing this small detail while in the witness stand?

The author Julian Symons conjectured that Camb pushed the pyjamas through the porthole after the body but forgot to mention it when he gave his police statement. When confronted with the need to explain their disappearance, he could say nothing. The problem with this conjecture is that Joshua Casswell saw his client the day before the trial. "If you got rid of them," he had told Camb, "you might as well say so." It would be an easy lie, like shooting at an open goal. No one could contradict him, and it would close up a problematic gap in his account. But Camb insisted he was telling the truth. Casswell was impressed that his client would not take the easy option, and was inclined to believe he was being honest.

Unfortunately for Camb, Casswell's instincts were correct. The explanatory gap was ruthlessly torn apart by the prosecution. When Roberts sat down, the glum faces on the defence table acknowledged his performance had been a tour de force. Camb's life was hanging in the balance.

In his closing speech, Casswell told the jury that Camb manoeuvred his body into the confined space between the chest of drawers and the bed {see photographic plates} while he was attempting to revive Gay. As he did so, he unknowingly hit the bell-pushes with his hip. If Camb had confirmed this in the witness box, it would have been the trump card for the defence – no one could refute the possibility and it would have engendered reasonable doubt. Yet, it was never put to Camb. Why?

When Casswell visited his client the day before the trial, it is inconceivable this was not discussed. He might have asked: "Can you remember if, at any time, you might have squeezed between the drawers and the bed?" Camb might have replied, as he did several times at the trial in response to other questions, "Not to my knowledge" or "I don't know". Such an equivocal response would hardly impress the jury and leave him to the mercy of Roberts in the cross-examination. Casswell might have decided to keep his powder dry, only advancing the argument in his closing speech for maximum effect.

Casswell also stressed that, if guilty of murder, the last thing Camb would have mentioned was the blood-stained froth that appeared on Gay's lips:

"For all he knew that was consistent with strangulation and no other form of death. But if, on the other hand, she died in his arms and froth came to her lips, is he not giving you just a picture of what happened? Something he would not have wanted to withhold because strangulation would not have entered his mind?"

Also, if Gay had been strangled, it is likely that other signs would have been present. These could include her face and neck turning blue due to low oxygen, a stippling effect on the skin as tiny blood vessels burst, particularly on the eyelids, and bloodshot eyes. Did

Camb have sufficient knowledge of medicine and forensics to recognise which symptoms he could and could not safely divulge?

Roberts closed for the prosecution. He meticulously ran through all the arguments he made during his brutal cross-examination: the lies, the bells ringing unaccountably, the missing black pyjamas and the motive for disposing of the body. He showed only contempt for Camb's account:

"He says he pushed her through the porthole in panic. Panic! Do you think he is the sort of man to panic? In the witness box, did you see any lack of poise, or composure, or full control of his thinking faculties? It was nothing more and nothing less than an act inspired by cold calculation induced by a desire for self-preservation, to destroy the whole of the evidence against him."

After Roberts sat down, the judge gave his charge to the jury. Within a few minutes, the defence feared the worst when he repeated the emotional rhetoric used by the prosecution: the body had been pushed "into shark-infested waters". It was agreed by the medical experts that Gay had died in her cabin, so the presence of sharks was quite irrelevant.

Most commentators agree that the judge's summing up was unfavourable to Camb, some claiming it was outright prejudiced. For example, regarding the forensic evidence of the prosecution, he stated that Dr Teare "was quite sure what he found is more consistent with death by strangulation", but failed to present clearly the conclusions of the defence experts. He neglected to state that Professor Webster believed natural death was more likely than strangulation. Instead, he merely described the four possible causes of natural death outlined by the professor.

Another example was Gay's romance with Charles Schwentafsky. The judge raised the question that, "If Miss Gibson was deeply in love with one man, is it likely that she would be inviting sexual intercourse with a deck steward with whom she had been acquainted for no more than a week?" Yet he failed to mention that she was easily infatuated – recall the strange affair with the army driver that developed in only two weeks – and Charles was hardly a priority in her life if she was travelling back to England to further her career. And why should he be? He was married.

The judge also explained the significance of the contraceptive found in Gay's suitcase:

"If a young woman has armed herself with a contraceptive against the risk of conception, and if she has waited in a dressing gown with nothing underneath, for the man with whom she expects to have sexual intercourse, it is hardly likely that she would not be wearing it at the time."

Does a contraceptive left in a suitcase point to murder? It depends. If Gay was pregnant there would be no point in using the diaphragm; the proverbial horse had bolted. On the other hand, if you believe Gay was on the liner only to further her acting career, and would have taken precautions if she had anticipated sex that night, the more you will doubt whether the actress was a consenting partner to the amorous intentions of the steward.

The black pyjamas were the last topic Mr Justice Hilbery covered in his speech. He repeated the prosecution's deadly logic:

"In the morning two things were missing, her dressing gown and the black pyjamas. Is the fact this: they were on and underneath the dressing gown, and they were never seen by the prisoner because there never was any sexual intercourse, and when he pushed her through the porthole he did not observe them because of the length of the dressing gown? Or is he telling the truth, and the black pyjamas are just missing articles, the disappearance of which is unexplained?"

At this point, James Camb must have realised that he had made a fatal mistake in not listening to his barrister about the significance of this evidence. The missing pyjamas were like a clue from an Agatha Christie novel, pointing the long finger of guilt at the prisoner in the dock, and made a lasting impression on everyone present.

At 6:30pm on Monday 22 March 1948, the judge asked the jury to consider its verdict. Only 45 minutes later, the jury of nine men and three women returned its verdict: guilty. There were gasps from the gallery, followed by occasional sobs and dabbing of eyes. When formally asked by the clerk why the court should not pass the death sentence, Camb replied: "My lord, at the opening of this case I was asked to plead guilty or not guilty. I pleaded not guilty, and I repeat that statement now." Mr Justice Hilbery placed a small black cloth on top of his wig and duly delivered the death sentence.

Geoffrey Roberts had won the personal duel. It was a rare defeat for Joshua Casswell. By the time he retired, after representing defendants in nearly 40 murder trials, only five were hanged. It was a remarkable record, but this was no comfort to James Camb and his family.

Legally, there was one last throw of the dice. Casswell appealed against the verdict on the grounds of misdirection by the judge; specifically, that Mr Justice Hilbery failed to put the defence case fairly in his charge to the jury. The Court of Criminal Appeal agreed the summing-up was unfavourable to the prisoner, but allowed that the judge was permitted to offer confident opinions upon questions of fact. There was no ground for interfering in the case and the appeal was dismissed on 26 April 1948.

A set of extraordinary circumstances now turned the wheel of fate. They had begun less than a week after Camb was charged with murder. On 31 October 1947, the Criminal Justice Bill received its first reading in the House of Commons. The bill removed from criminal law some extreme punishments, such as hard labour and corporal punishment. Anxious to assuage the large number of its backbenchers who felt strongly about the issue, the Labour Government indicated it might allow a free vote on the abolition of the death penalty if an amendment was tabled.

On 21 November, three days before Camb was committed for trial, a motion was announced by backbench Labour MP Sydney Silverman to amend the Criminal Justice Bill, suspending the death penalty for five years. Its proponents believed the suspension would show that the deterrent effect of capital punishment was specious, reflecting the experience of other countries that had abolished the death penalty without an increase in the murder rate. It was hoped this would pave the way for its permanent abolition.

Despite heated debate in Parliament and the national press, the death penalty remained in force. On 16 January 1948, Walter John Cross was convicted of strangling a disabled watchmaker two months before, and the 21-year-old lorry driver was sentenced to death. The Court of Criminal Appeal upheld the conviction on 2 February and his execution followed two weeks later. The well-oiled British justice system was brutal in its efficiency. It had taken less than three months from the commission of the crime to the execution of its perpetrator. Almost certainly, Camb would have stepped onto the gallows had his original trial date not been postponed from December 1947.

Four days after Camb was found guilty of murder, on 26 March 1948, the Silverman motion was tabled during the second reading of the Criminal Justice Bill. On 14 April, the motion was passed by the House of Commons on a free vote, suspending the death penalty for five years. The Home Secretary announced that it would be abhorrent to execute prisoners after the vote but before the bill became law. Starting immediately, death sentences would be automatically commuted to life prison sentences.

A week later, 22-year-old Donald Thomas was found guilty of murdering PC Nathaniel Edgar. It was the first murder trial since the vote to suspend capital punishment. Usual courtroom practice was also suspended, most noticeably the judge did not wear the customary black cap when passing the death sentence on the former soldier. The Home Secretary, James Chuter Ede, commuted the sentence to life imprisonment. A few days later, Camb discovered he too had escaped the noose.

By the time the House of Lords debated the Criminal Justice Bill on 2 June, four convicted murderers had been spared a trip to the gallows. After two days of debate, however, the second chamber overturned the decision of the House of Commons, deleting the motion to suspend the death penalty from the bill. The Government responded by drafting a compromise position in which the death penalty was retained only for certain categories of murder committed with "express malice". When the new clause was put before the Commons, Winston Churchill was scathing:

"It has been put together not with the object of making a better and more humane system of criminal justice, but of getting around an awkward cabinet or parliamentary difficulty. The attorney-general said it was a compromise. Confusion is not compromise. A bargain between politicians in difficulties ought not to be the basis of our criminal law… the House of Commons has, by its vote, saved the life of the brutal lascivious murderer who thrust the poor girl he had raped and assaulted through a porthole of the ship to the sharks."

The rhetoric eclipsed the facts. It also failed to persuade anyone. The compromise clause was passed by the Commons on 15 July. As expected, the House of Lords rejected it after "tearing it to shreds" during another impassioned debate. On 23 July the Criminal Justice Bill, without the clause to suspend the death penalty, was passed by the House of Commons and became law a week later. The moratorium on executions was lifted, and the death penalty remained in force for a further 17 years.

Members of the Cold Case Jury, we have examined the events leading up the death of Gay Gibson, how Camb lied to the captain and the police, the testimony presented at his trial and how the wrangling over the death penalty in Parliament saved his life. But what really occurred in cabin 126 as the liner steamed off the coast of West Africa? We now return to the decks of the *Durban Castle* to reconstruct the events of the early hours of Saturday 18 October 1947, with two different versions of what might have taken place.

Chapter 9

IMPROPER LIAISONS

The following reconstruction shows the most likely chain of events if Gay Gibson's death was a case of misadventure. It is written from Camb's perspective and based on his testimony, witness statements and the arguments of his lawyers.

We rewind time to the final hour of Friday 17 October 1947 on board the *Durban Castle*. The evening's dinner dance has ended and Camb is busy serving the last rounds of drinks before the bar closes.

11:10pm The elderly passenger fanned herself with a Union Castle brochure. For the past six nights she had sat in the same place in the Long Gallery and each night she had complained of a different ache or pain that prevented her from sleeping well, and for which the self-prescribed remedy was always the same – gin and tonic. The correct dose: several of them. Camb was only too happy to oblige, as she was the best tipper on the voyage.

"How much longer do we have to tolerate this infernal heat?" she complained in her high-pitched and pinched public school accent. "It must be over 80 degrees."

"Not much longer," Camb replied reassuringly. "We're in the tropics now but as we head north the temperature will cool, and by the time we dock at Southampton you will be positively shivering, I promise."

"I will be happy if it snows!"

As she spoke, Gay Gibson swept into the Long Gallery from the Smoke Room. She looked stunning: her sleeveless, black evening dress contrasted with the paleness of her skin, and a swirling gold-patterned bodice highlighted her waist and curvaceous figure. Her bob of luxurious auburn hair settled on a wide fold-over neckline of black velvet. Her gaze fixed straight ahead, she was unaware of the deck steward, although he had certainly noticed her.

"Well, it's impossible to sleep in this heat," the passenger continued, "quite impossible."

"Excuse me for one minute," Camb interrupted deferentially and walked briskly to catch up with Gay.

"I've got a bone to pick with you. And a big one at that." Hurrying by, the senior nightwatchman, James Murray, was shocked to hear a deck steward speaking so familiarly with a first-class passenger.

Gay immediately spun round to see Camb smiling broadly. He observed her eyes scanning his body. He knew he looked good in his more casual evening attire, his white sleeveless shirt framing his bronzed and muscular arms.

"And what would that be?" she replied, puzzled.

"You did not use your tea tray last night, nor this afternoon. I had them prepared, as usual."

"Oh, there was nothing wrong with the tea service. After drinking the rum last night I didn't feel like having tea. It was too hot, anyhow. And this afternoon, I dozed off."

"And tonight?"

"I would like another rum, please. I really must dash. I need my swimsuit." She turned, took several steps before glancing over her shoulder. For a moment Camb was spellbound, unable to respond. He was mesmerised by the swirl of auburn hair and the sparkle in her brown eyes. It was a sensual look, provocative and potent. It beckoned to him, stoking a fire of desire. He visualised the black evening dress falling to the floor, revealing the curves of her naked body.

Then she was gone. The spell broken, he remembered the customer he had left abruptly. Knowing exactly what she would want, he popped into the bar and emerged a minute later. "There's only one thing that helps me sleep when it's this hot," he said, placing a drink on the table. "A large gin and tonic." The passenger beamed. Camb took payment and a generous tip, but his charm was so instilled that his actions had been an unthinking reflex. His mind was elsewhere, weighing up his next move.

Throughout the voyage, he had avoided visiting Gay's cabin at night, but now he felt compelled to go. Avoiding eye contact with everyone in the Long Gallery, Camb quietly stepped outside, stopping by the door of the Deck Pantry, and scanned the starboard side for any other crew members. Confident he was not being observed, he quickly headed down two decks and within a couple of minutes was outside cabin 126.

11:20pm He knocked gently on the door, which half-opened. Gay was surprised. "Oh! I didn't think you were allowed down here?" There was a teasing, playful tone to her voice. She swung the door open and returned to the ransacked suitcase on her bed. "I cannot find my swimsuit anywhere. I know I packed it." Camb quietly entered the cabin. "Anyway, what can I do for you?" she asked, without turning around.

"I wondered if you would like some lemonade with your rum."

"It's a long way to come just to ask me that," she giggled. "I don't, thank you."

Not wanting to leave, but not knowing what to say, there was an uncomfortable silence while Camb stood dumbly watching Gay delving into her suitcase.

"Do you know what?" he asked finally.

Gay straightened up and faced him. "What?"

"I've a good mind to bring a drink down and join you later."

"Please yourself," she said enticingly. "It's up to you."

For Camb, the meaning of those words could not have been clearer. Why else would she be amenable to him returning to her cabin so late at night? The steward could barely control himself. He wanted to reach out and sweep his left hand down the cascade of her hair, pull her close, kiss her. He dared not. Not yet. "I'd better get back now," he said quietly, "otherwise I might be missed." He left, walking back quickly to his deck duties.

12:55am Camb finished stowing the deck chairs in the locker on the starboard side of Promenade Deck. He returned to the pantry to lock up and then took the few steps into the bar. He headed straight for the bottle box. The large glass of rum he placed there for Gay was gone, but curiously in its place was a small alarm clock. He glanced outside, and saw Gay alone on deck. Still in her evening dress, she was leaning back against the rail, a cigarette holder in her right hand and the glass of rum in the other. She was watching him closely. He picked up the clock and walked outside.

"Is this yours?" Camb asked, perplexed.

Gay blew a column of smoke above his head. "It is," she replied. Without averting her gaze from the deck steward, she removed the cigarette holder from her lips and tapped some ash onto the deck.

"You shouldn't leave it there or you might forget it."

She smiled and, transferring the glass into her right hand, outstretched her left palm into which Camb placed the alarm clock. "Thank you."

"I'm just finishing up," he explained. Leaving Gay standing by the railing, he darted into the Long Gallery. By the time he had arranged the chairs neatly under the tables, switched off the lights and returned to the deck, Gay had gone. He hurried down to B Deck, adrenalin surging through his veins. The door to cabin 126 was shut but, from the grilled vent above the door, a soft light diffused into the alleyway, casting linear patterns on the ceiling and walls. He knocked and waited. Surprised by the lack of an answer, he cautiously opened the door and peered inside. The bedside light softly illuminated the empty cabin like candlelight. Closing the door quietly, he waited outside. Two minutes passed, perhaps three. Where on earth was she? Anxious that if he stayed any longer he might be seen, the deck steward left.

He went to the crew area, where he found himself alone in a corner of the Well Deck. A lit cigarette in hand, he lay back against a bulkhead. There was silence, except for the constant engine rumble and a distant echo of waves breaking against the hull. He looked up at the night sky, a few smudges of grey against a string of brilliant lights, but he saw only Gay, her face imprinted onto his consciousness like an after-image.

Camb decided not to rush back. He wanted to allow Gay ample time to finish whatever she was doing and prepare for bed. She might even be having a bath, he surmised, to cool down and freshen up. By the time he decided to leave the Well Deck there were three cigarette butts stubbed out beside him. He stood up, lightly brushed himself down, and headed for cabin 126 once again.

2:10am Running his hand through his hair, Camb approached the door. He knocked gently and opened it. His heart raced. There she was, reclined on the bed, wearing a full-length, yellow dressing gown. He closed the door and, not wanting to signal his intentions coarsely, left it unbolted.

"Well," he declared, sitting on the edge of the bed, "perhaps you can tell me what happened at the scintillating dinner dance this evening. Did Bray dance with you like a father?"

Gay giggled. "No."

"He didn't dance with you?"

"Yes he did, twice, but not like a father." She paused. "More like an uncle." They laughed. "We ought to keep our voices down a bit," she warned, pointing to the far wall. "There is a passenger in the next cabin. Mind you, she might not be able to hear much – she looks as old as Jericho!" They laughed again. The conversation ambled around the dinner dance and the boredom of the voyage, with the occasional joke at the expense of her two dining companions. Throughout, Camb was biding his time, waiting for the right moment to make his move.

2:25am He leaned forward and wrapped his hand around hers. A frisson of sexual charge sparked between them. He glanced towards the door. "We'd better lock it."

She smiled. "That doesn't matter. No one will come in."

Camb moved forward, sweeping his hand through her hair and down to the nape of her neck, pulling her face tenderly towards his until their lips met. She was a little hesitant at first, her initial kisses light, almost exploratory. Then desire overwhelmed control. Their mouths parted, tongues entwined, passionate hands feeling each other. She caressed the side of his face with one hand, while the other slowly unzipped the front of her dressing gown as far as her naval. Underneath, she was naked.

He was stunned by her beauty. Her skin was flawless, the most milky white he had ever seen, her breasts pert and ample. His left hand slid over her right breast, his mouth licking the light brown areola of the other. Gay threw her head back, exhaling deeply. Sexual power surging, Camb felt himself stiffening. He moved his right hand down to her waist and finding the zip, slowly pushed it down as far as it would go, the dressing gown opening like a flower. The vulnerability Gay now felt was indescribably erotic; she was in the hands of this wild and strong stranger. Her pulse skyrocketed. She moved her legs apart, as he continually kissed her stomach, teasingly heading downwards, until she gasped.

Camb moved his body over Gay's, placing his left arm under her neck. Gay closed her eyes as he slipped deep inside. Cradling her right arm around the nape of his neck, her left hand squeezed his forearm. His thrusting was frantic, almost angry. Gay felt an intense, warm pressure from the constant movement. Emotional and physical pleasure intermingled until they were indistinguishable, the intensity continuously building. Her heart beat faster and faster. She could hear her lover beginning to groan, his actions more forceful than ever, the pressure inside her ever growing. Her whole body started to quiver, her stomach clenched, and her back started to arch on the inexorable rise to climax.

2:40am Then it happened. Instinctively, she knew something was terribly wrong. Like a machine out of control, her heart felt like it was shaking itself to pieces; a pain so extreme that she feared her chest would burst. Her lungs started to burn as if they were filling with acid. She feared every bone in her body would snap as all her muscles seemed to warp and contract. Her body heaved, her arm tightening around Camb's neck like a boa. He winced as her fingernails sank into his right forearm like claws. He thought she was playing rough; he rode her even harder.

As suddenly as the pain had ripped through her body, it lost its intensity. Gay felt woozy, anaesthetised, as if her mind was spinning in another dimension outside of reality. A dimension in which there was no sound. In which everything was blurred. In which she could no longer feel anything.

Camb felt her entire body relax under him. Her grip on his forearm eased, the arm around his neck unwound and limply fell, hanging off the side of the bed like a broken branch. Bubbles of muddy-coloured saliva flecked with blood oozed from her lips. Her right eye was almost completely shut. The other had a stone-cold stare.

"Gay? Are you all right?"

Alarmed, he jumped off the bed and hurriedly put on his clothes to fetch medical help. As his hand grabbed the doorknob he stopped. The quickest way to end his career would be to get the ship's doctor. He would be immediately discharged under the worst possible circumstances. His life on the high seas, his life of adulterous adventure and excitement, would be over. It would be the monotony of an office job for the rest of his career. How he had loathed his old factory job. He had only lasted as long as five months to please his wife. And, despite his infidelities, he loved her still. If he was discharged in these circumstances, his marriage would be over too.

Fear gripped him. "Get out now!" his inner voice was telling him, but he could not leave her like this. He was not a monster. He loosened his grip on the door and turned to face the bed. If he could not get help, he must try to revive her. He spotted the vanity bag on top of the chest of drawers. He opened it, frantically picking over the cosmetics and toiletries in an attempt to find smelling salts, but there was nothing he could use. In his clumsy panic, he knocked the alarm clock onto the floor. In the adjoining cabin, Mrs Stephens, who was not quite as old as Jericho, awoke with the crashing sound, believing someone had dropped a tray. Thinking nothing of it, she rolled over and went back to sleep.

Camb bent over the still body. He pressed his ear to her naked chest but there was no heartbeat. With the heel of his palm, he massaged her chest, hoping to bring life back to her veins. After several minutes, when he saw there was no change in her condition, his panic escalated. "Come on, Gay!" The more futile the situation became, the more vigorously he pounded her chest. Anyone could see that life had fled, but he continued just the same. Exhausted, he finally stopped and caught his breath. He picked up the alarm clock and replaced it on the chest of drawers.

2:58am In utter desperation, and still not thinking properly, he attempted artificial respiration. To reach her mouth, he squeezed his body into the narrow space between the bed and drawers. Tired and fraught, he was unaware that his left hip had pressed against the bottom two push-buttons on the wall. It was only for a second, perhaps a second and a half, but long enough to change his life.

An electrical charge surged through the cables to the first-class pantry on the deck below. The ringing bells gave Frederick Steer a jolt. Jumping up, he threw his magazine onto the table, walked into the adjacent first-class dining room and took the steps that led to the first-class entrance hall on B Deck. He turned right and looked at the indicator board on the wall. Both the red and green lights were illuminated for the portside galley. This was unusual, possibly indicating a problem. He hurried along the portside corridor.

2:59am Steer turned and entered the small alleyway. On the far wall both call lights for cabin 126 were illuminated. He quickly reached the cabin and knocked on the door. Inside, Camb turned. In terror, he saw the door opening. He forced it shut with the palm of his hand and bolted it. "All right," he called out. Steer was shocked. The door had only opened a couple of inches before it was slammed in his face, but it was enough for him to glimpse a dark-haired man dressed in a white sleeveless shirt and blue trousers standing by the bed. He knew who it was. He turned and hurried back to A Deck.

Frozen with fear, Camb stood motionless in the centre of the cabin. His concern was no longer for the dead girl lying on the bed. After all, he rationalised, she could no longer be helped, but he was in big trouble. He did not believe he had been recognised, but that was of no help. Someone was waiting in the passageway, almost certainly a crew member. If he left the cabin now he would be accosted. Even if he told the truth, he would be sacked for being inside a passenger's cabin. And who would believe that a young woman could die so suddenly, so mysteriously? He might even be accused of murder. No, the truth was his enemy.

Panic rising, Camb's mouth was dry, his hands shaking. The more he thought about it, the more he saw there was no way out. The nightwatchman would report that someone was inside the cabin.

Even if he managed to flee the scene without notice, he was sure to be the prime suspect if he left the body on the bed. Like Marley's Ghost, his reputation for misdeeds and improper liaisons had forged long chains that now shackled him. He was a prisoner of karma.

Looking round the cabin, he eyed the porthole. His instinct for self-preservation firmly back in control, the idea struck him: what if her body was never found? What if she had fallen overboard? She had been seen alone by the deck railings after consuming several alcoholic drinks. If he was apprehended outside the cabin, he could say: "She's not here. I don't know where she is." Perhaps he could even invent a story that she had been suicidal and, concerned, he was checking to see if she was safe in her cabin. It was a long shot, but anything was better than the truth. It might just save his career and his neck. Decision made, he switched on the main cabin light.

3:04am "Are you certain you saw Camb?" James Murray asked, as the two watchmen hurried down the B Deck corridor.

"It was definitely Camb, sir," replied Steer.

Murray placed his finger to his lips as they approached the alleyway and tiptoed to cabin 126. He turned off both bell lights outside the cabin. Inside, Camb heard the faint click. Alerted that someone was outside, he froze, barely breathing. Murray looked at the grille above the door and noted that the cabin light was on.

Keeping his ear pressed to the cabin door, Camb waited for several minutes. When he was satisfied whoever was outside had left, he leapt onto the bed like an athlete. Straddling the body, he dragged it towards him then heaved it into a sitting position against the outside wall below the open porthole. Still wearing her yellow dressing gown and with her head drooping to one side, Gay looked less human, more rag doll. It made his task easier.

As he stood by the porthole, a faint breeze diffused into the cabin and he could hear gushing water from the bilge pumps below. Grabbing the body at the waist, he offered it up to the opening like a ritual sacrifice. Struggling with the dead weight of a limp body, he summoned enormous physical effort. He managed to push her arms through the porthole first, followed by her head and shoulders. At just under half a metre in diameter, the porthole was an extremely tight squeeze. Another large push and her torso followed. Resting on her stomach, her head, arms and upper body were hanging outside the cabin while her hips and legs were dangling inside, acting as a counterweight.

The final part was relatively easy. Camb crouched down on the bed, grabbed hold of her legs, and bench-pressed them above his head. As the legs rose above the bottom of the porthole, gravity took over. Her legs shot out of the cabin as the body fell the height of a house into the hungry sea below. There was a splash, but nothing that the bridge would hear over the bow wave. Camb quickly straightened the sheets, turned off the lights, and pressed his ear against the door again. He could hear nothing. He quietly opened the door and walked out. To his relief, no one was there.

*

Members of the Cold Case Jury, the utter selfishness of James Camb is appalling. Even his defence barrister, the charitable and open-minded Joshua Casswell, never forgave the callousness of his client for throwing a body overboard. Yet, despite his revulsion and dislike, he wrote in his memoir, "I was inclined to think at the time that my client's story was true and, on balance, I still think so." Like Casswell, your natural disgust at how Camb disposed of the young woman's dead body should not colour your judgement. Let us look at the evidence.

What natural cause could possibly trigger the death of a young woman in this way? Following the medical testimony at the trial, the reconstruction assumes it was heart failure, possibly cardiac arrhythmia. This is not a heart attack, in which the flow of blood to the heart muscle is blocked, but when electrical signals to the heart malfunction, causing it to beat uncontrollably fast and the ventricles to quiver or spasm. Death is sudden, typically without warning. It may be triggered by an underlying condition but, even after an autopsy, no cause may be discovered.

The chief officer of the *Durban Castle* recalled it was "a terribly hot, humid night. You could hardly get your breath, and it was worse in the cabins." Gay was hospitalised with a chronic ear condition three weeks before she left for South Africa, and this was picked up by her army medical. According to Professor James Webster's testimony, any "septic focus" in the body can infect the heart, in particular the specialised heart muscles that form part of its natural pacemaker. Physical effort, particularly in demanding climatic conditions, could trigger heart failure.

Eleven years after the trial, Webster claimed he had evidence affirming his opinion that Gay Gibson was not a healthy young woman when she boarded the *Durban Castle*. "You Did Not Kill Gay Gibson" was the front-page headline of the *Sunday Pictorial* on 13 September 1959 {see *Exhibit F*}. He proclaimed, "I now have reason to believe Gay Gibson was suffering from chronically poisoned tonsils. This set up a condition called toxic myocarditis – a disease of the heart muscles." It is believed that up to one in five of all cases of sudden death in young adults are due to myocarditis. Symptoms sometimes include shortness of breath, chest pain, light-headedness, irregular heartbeat and sudden loss of consciousness.

At the trial, Webster cited his personal involvement with the case of a seven-year-old boy who died pushing his bicycle up a hill. The apparently healthy lad died because an infected left tonsil poisoned his heart muscles. Now Webster was claiming the same had killed Gay Gibson, but where was his evidence? The report did not say. However, Gay's singing teacher in Johannesburg observed that she had a yellow-headed lump in the back of her throat and feared it was tuberculosis. Webster might have believed it was more likely to be poisoned tonsils. But there is a problem: Gay's tonsils were removed when she was 11 years old. It is possible the beds of tissue at the back of her throat became infected, but it remains a surprisingly speculative theory.

Gay always bolted her cabin door at night because she felt alone and vulnerable on the sparsely occupied liner. This was confirmed by Frank Hopwood, who accompanied her to her cabin late each night, and the stewardess Eileen Field, who delivered orange juice to her cabin early each morning. If Camb was welcome, what was Gay expecting at that time of night? It is difficult to believe she was anticipating a late-night conversation about philosophy or art. If he was not welcome, and the door bolted, how did Camb get into her cabin?

A crucial factor in the case is the ringing of the bells. A steward or stewardess was summoned to a cabin by pushing the appropriate button on the bedside panel. The push-buttons were situated on the bulkhead or wall, about a metre above the deck, between the bed and the chest of drawers. It was a narrow gap – about 30cm between bed and chest – but wide enough for a person to squeeze into. The three buttons were close together, protruding without any beading or edging, so that an accidental push of two together was possible.

After 10pm, a nightwatchman would be summoned, regardless of the button pushed. Bells would ring in the pantry on A Deck, where the nightwatchmen worked. A series of lights on the deck, the corridor, the alleyway and outside the door of the calling cabin would illuminate {see *Exhibits A and B*}. Only when a nightwatchman followed this Hansel-and-Gretel-like trail of lights would he know which cabin had rung for assistance. After arriving, his first action was typically to extinguish the entire chain by depressing the illuminated light or lights and then knock on the appropriate cabin door. Inside the cabin, there was no indication that anyone had been summoned. Without pushing the buttons yourself, the only way to know was to observe someone else pressing them, or peering outside the cabin door to see if the lights were on.

In his police statement and at his trial, Camb said he definitely did not touch the bell-pushes. The court heard from the ship's electrician that the bells and cabling were tested at Southampton and were found to be working normally. No instances of malfunction had been reported. The prosecution contended this implied that the bell-pushes must have been pressed by one of the two people in the cabin. If it was definitely not Camb then it must have been Gay Gibson and, since two buttons were pushed at the same time, this was done deliberately, an urgent cry for help.

It was unusual for both a steward and stewardess to be summoned simultaneously, but this does not imply that both buttons were pushed intentionally. In *The Porthole Murder Case*, Denis Herbstein recounts that during a subsequent voyage, a first-class passenger lying on the bed, reading and smoking, stretched across to an ashtray on top of the chest of drawers. Unaware that her hand had brushed against the two buttons, both the steward and stewardess were summoned. In cabin 126 that night, were both buttons pressed unknowingly by Camb?

The prosecution's assertion might be correct, however. Gay Gibson might have pushed both buttons frantically, perhaps one after the other, to summon help. This possibility is central to the theory that she was murdered. It is to this theory that we now turn.

Chapter 10
FATAL MISTAKE

The next reconstruction closely follows the central claim of the prosecution at the trial. It is written from Gay's perspective and assumes she had no amorous inclinations towards the narcissistic deck steward. Let us again rewind time to Friday 17 October 1947. The dinner dance has ended and Gay Gibson is in the Smoke Room talking to her dining companions.

11:10pm "You were the belle of the ball, Miss Gibson," said the squadron leader. "Your silver shoes lit up the whole deck." Bray placed his glass on the circular table in the centre of the three armchairs occupied by the dining companions.

Gay smiled politely. It was hard not to stand out, she thought, given everyone else had to be at least twice her age. Nevertheless, she appreciated the attention.

"Now, what about this night swim of yours?" Frank Hopwood asked.

"Yes, it's so dreadfully hot, I would like to have a dip in the pool," replied Gay, rising from her chair. "I'll fetch my swimsuit. Please excuse me." The two gentlemen also stood up.

"Shall I accompany you?"

"I'll be fine, Mr Hopwood. Thank you." The paternal attention was well-meaning but, after a week, it was beginning to grate. As she left, dressed in an elegant black dress that highlighted her curvaceous figure, she drew discreet glances from many of the men. She walked confidently into the Long Gallery.

"I have a bone to pick with you," pronounced the stern voice. She stopped and turned to see James Camb standing behind her, smiling impishly. "And a big one at that," he added, his smile broadening.

"And what would that be?" she replied, puzzled.

"You did not use your tea tray last night, nor this afternoon. I had them prepared, as usual."

"Oh, there was nothing wrong with the tea service. After drinking the rum last night I didn't feel like having tea. It was too hot, anyhow. And this afternoon, I dozed off."

"And tonight?"

She thought he was fussing unnecessarily, but replied politely, "I would like another rum, please." Not wanting to talk, she added. "I really must dash. I need my swimsuit." She noted a trace of disappointment in the steward's expression, who clearly was hoping for a longer conversation. Walking the few steps towards the double doors leading to the port side of Promenade Deck, she thought she heard one of her companions calling after her. Glancing briefly over her shoulder, she realised she was mistaken, and continued on her way.

11:20pm Back in her cabin, Gay lifted her suitcase onto the bed, unzipped it and started to rummage through its contents. It was not long before she was disturbed by a knock on the door. She opened it halfway and was surprised to see Camb standing there.

"Oh? I didn't think you were allowed down here," she remarked pleasantly, although she really was not interested in stewarding etiquette. She fully opened the door and resumed her search. "I cannot find my swimsuit anywhere. I know I packed it. Anyway, what can I do for you?"

"I wondered if you would like some lemonade with your rum."

"It's a long way to come just to ask me that," she laughed. She knew the steward was paying her too much attention, but found it flattering. "I don't, thank you."

Camb fell silent. She sensed his eyes were fixed on her as she bent over her suitcase. The awkwardness was broken when he asked: "Do you know what?"

Gay straightened up and faced him. "What?"

"I've got a good mind to get a drink and join you later."

"Well, that might land you in hot water," she said coolly, her mind preoccupied by her missing swimsuit. Camb looked distant, distracted, but she thought nothing of it. She opened the wardrobe door.

"I'd better get back now," he said quietly. "Otherwise, I might be missed."

When she closed the wardrobe, he was gone. After making a final, unsuccessful search for the swimsuit, Gay gave up, frustrated. Despite the sweltering heat, she could not cool off in the pool. Sighing, she sat on the edge of her bed, her thoughts wandering. She took a bundle of letters from the alcove above her bed. One, tied with a pink ribbon bow, was put to one side while she glanced over the letters of introduction. She had read them many times, but never tired of the promise they held. She was most excited by the possibility of working at the Abbey Theatre in Dublin. Her mother believed if she obtained a position there, she could act anywhere, even Hollywood. That was the dream, but at what cost? She picked up the special letter, and kissed it. "I miss you, Charles," she said softly. She sat silently for several minutes, re-reading every line and reminiscing about the most exciting time of her life, the time spent with him in Johannesburg and Durban. "Write soon, my love." With a final kiss, she replaced the bundle of letters and left her cabin.

11:50pm After agreeing it was too hot and stuffy to retire to their cabins, the three companions moved to the outside deck. They leaned over the rails, trying to catch the sea breeze, and talked sporadically.

"Resignedly beneath the sky, the melancholy waters lie," Gay uttered theatrically.

"Edgar Allan Poe," the squadron leader remarked, impressed. "Although I cannot for the life of me remember the poem's title."

"*City in the Sea*, I think."

"Ah, yes."

For nearly an hour they talked. The conversation ebbed and flowed as they discussed poetry and novels about the sea, Gay's theatre anecdotes and more about her career plans. Mostly the latter.

"I think it's time we turned in, don't you?" Hopwood suggested finally. "It's Saturday now."

"Oh, that's a shame, I loved Friday!" Gay gushed. "It was the best day of the voyage so far." The passengers ambled across the deck before descending. As usual, Hopwood escorted Gay back to her room, bade her sweet dreams and left.

12:55am Her cabin too hot for sleep, Gay was on Promenade Deck for some cool air and alcohol. Having been ushered away from the stern of the ship by the boatswain's mate swabbing down the deck, she leaned against the rail opposite the Long Gallery, looking through the double doors. She saw Camb inside, standing at the bar and looking quizzically at her clock. He glanced up.

"Is this yours?" he asked, striding outside onto the deck.

Gay blew a column of smoke above his head. "It is," she replied, removing the cigarette holder from her lips and tapping some ash onto the deck.

"You shouldn't leave it there or you might forget it."

"Thank you." It was obvious he liked her, perhaps a bit too much, but she saw no harm in it. His attentions were merely a distraction on a long voyage, nothing more.

"I'm just finishing up," he said, walking back inside. Seeing the working party had moved on, she moved back down the deck to the veranda that overlooked the pool. Placing the clock next to her, she sat on a wicker sofa affording views to starboard. It gave her a tingle to think that on the horizon, hiding in the dark, was exotic western Africa. She sat alone, slowly sipping her rum, enjoying the tranquillity of a tropical night.

1:20am She watched the reflections of the deck lights shimmer on the surface of the pool like dancing ghosts and heard the breaking bow wave as the liner steamed into the night. They reminded her of refreshing, cool water. If she could not have a swim, she would have a long bath. She rose from the sofa, the glass of rum in one hand and cigarette holder in the other, and headed down decks. Forgotten, the brown alarm clock was left behind. It faithfully kept time, ticking down the last two hours of Gay's life.

Within ten minutes, Gay's naked body was submerged beneath lukewarm bath water. For the first time she did not feel stickily hot and uncomfortable. She slowly drank her rum. She was sure the deck steward had given her a double, and she appreciated it now. There were advantages in attracting male attention, she mused.

2:30am Her wrinkled fingers and toes told her she had bathed long enough. Stepping out of the bath, she dried herself before pulling on her silk pyjamas and lemon dressing gown, which she zipped up the front, but only about three quarters of the way. She walked the short distance back to the heat of her cabin, bolted the door behind her and picked up *My Life in Art* from the alcove next to her bed. Lying back on the bed, the book fell open at a chapter titled "The Seagull", about the production of Chekhov's play, and she was quickly engrossed.

2:40am A tap at the door was followed by a rattling of the handle. Alarmed, Gay sat upright and nervously looked towards the door.

"Who is it?" she whispered.

ABOVE This studio shot of Gay Gibson was taken in South Africa a few weeks before she died. She appears a picture of health, but what was causing her to tire easily, turn blue and faint?

LEFT The hull of the *Durban Castle*. Gay Gibson was pushed through the third porthole from the left, falling 25 feet to the sea, where she was lost to the deep.

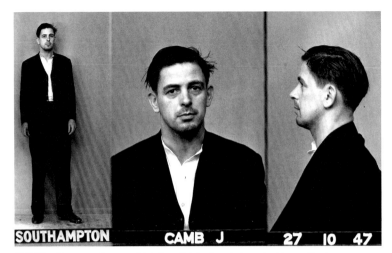

ABOVE Looking worse for wear, this is the official police photograph of James Camb, the day after he was charged with the murder of Gay Gibson.

BELOW James Camb's left palm print matched the one lifted from inside the door of Cabin 126.

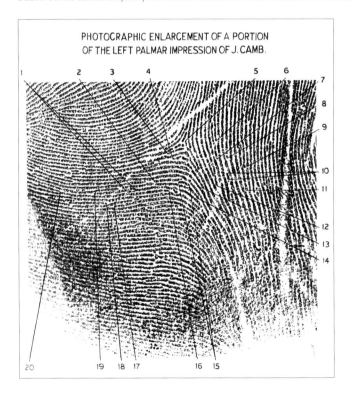

PHOTOGRAPHIC ENLARGEMENT OF A PORTION
OF THE LEFT PALMAR IMPRESSION OF J. CAMB.

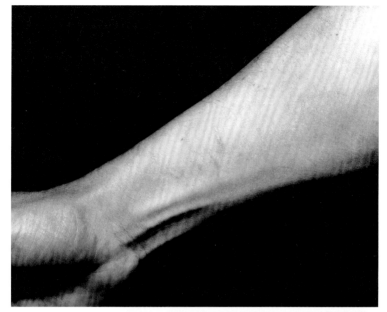

ABOVE Injuries to Camb's right wrist. According to Dr Griffiths, when he saw the injuries, they contained "red weals of inflammation" and were no more than two days old.

RIGHT Injuries to Camb's left shoulder. Dr Griffiths accepted these were caused by Camb scratching in bed due to the heat of the tropics.

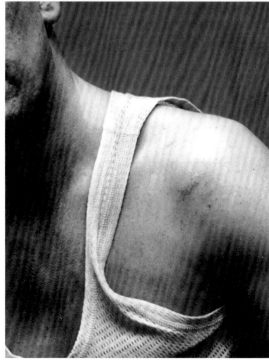

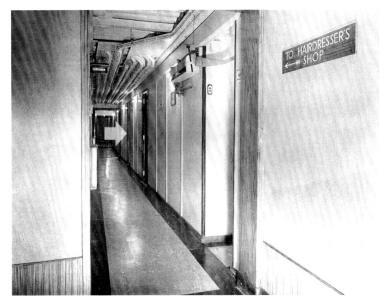

ABOVE The portside corridor, B Deck. The entrance to the alleyway leading to Cabin 126 is arrowed

BELOW Cabin 126 as it appeared at midday on Saturday 18 October 1947. Note the porthole is close to the bed. In the alcove is a copy of *My Life In Art*.

ABOVE The bedside panel is between the bed and the chest of drawers. The top switch turned on the cylindrical reading light, the middle button summoned the steward, and the bottom the stewardess. How were these two buttons pressed at 2:58am on 18 October 1947?

BELOW Cabin 126 as it appeared at 7:30am on Saturday 18 October 1947; the bed had been ruffled by Eileen Field for the police photograph. It appears Gay's luggage was moved into her room after she had disappeared.

ABOVE The plywood court inside the historic Great Hall at Winchester.

BELOW The bed and door from Cabin 126 and a replica of the porthole before they were taken into court.

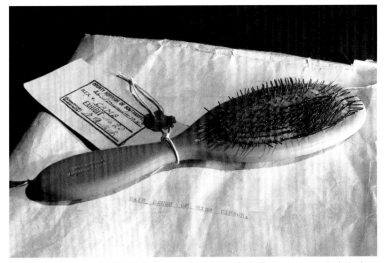

ABOVE Gay's hairbrush was Exhibit 20 at James Camb's trial. Dr Griffiths was never asked whether it could have caused the fine scratches found on the back of Camb's neck. (Image © BBC).

BELOW Front left, Frank Hopwood, one of Gay's dining companions. Right, Eileen Field, the stewardess who discovered Gay was missing. Back left, Fred Steer, the nightwatchman. When the bells rang, did he rush directly to Cabin 126, or did he take longer than he claimed?
(Image © MirrorPix).

LEFT Daisy Gibson walks to court to resolutely defend her daughter's reputation. She told the court that Gay "was one of the finest types of English womanhood".

BELOW James Camb, his face carefully obscured, poses for the serialisation of his story in the *Sunday Pictorial*. He enjoyed 12 years of freedom before being imprisoned again in 1971.
(Both images © MirrorPix).

"It's Jimmy," the voice was hushed and muffled. "You forgot your alarm clock." She glanced at her chest of drawers – the clock was missing. "You left it on the veranda."

"Oh, yes. One moment, please." Closing her book, she returned it to the alcove. Zipping her dressing gown to the top, she rose, slid back the bolt, and pulled the door ajar.

"I thought you might need it tomorrow morning," Camb smiled, handing her the clock.

"Thank you for taking the trouble to return it. That was kind of you." When there was no response, she added, "Goodnight, then," and slowly closed the door, but was surprised to encounter resistance. With his foot firmly placed against the bottom of the door, Camb kept it open.

"May I come in? I would like to talk."

"It's a little late…"

"If I stand here I might be seen or wake someone."

Gay appreciated his favour, and supposed he was as hot and bored as she was and only wanted a chat. "All right, but it can't be for long. You know you should not be down here." She pulled open the door. It was a fatal mistake.

Once inside, Camb presumptuously sat at the end of her bed. Gay closed the door, leaving it unbolted, and returned the alarm clock to its appointed place on the drawers. She leaned against the plumped-up pillows at the head of her bed, wrapped her hands around her drawn-up legs, and rested her chin on her knees.

Camb talked about the dinner dance and moved onto stories about some of the crew members. Gay started to relax. Unfurling her legs, she stretched out on the bed, talking enthusiastically about her stage career and her hopes for the future.

2:28am Without warning, Camb abruptly changed the conversation. "I think you're beautiful." He moved rapidly, lying fully on top of her. Gay was immobilised by the weight of the well-built steward.

"What are you doing?" She exclaimed, repulsed by the smell of stale cigarette smoke and sweat as his face rubbed up against hers. He repeatedly kissed her face and lips. Straining, she attempted to throw him off, but it was futile. His right hand slid over her left breast. "Get off!" she hissed. "I have a boyfriend!"

Stroking her hair, Camb shifted his weight to his left. Gay gasped for breath as the air was squeezed from her lungs. She could barely talk, let alone shout. With his right hand, he started to slowly unzip her dressing gown, while his left hand firmly held her face. A fear that she had never known surged through her body: if he was not stopped, she would be raped.

Unable to prise her face away from his grip, she blindly flung her right arm outwards and backwards in the direction of the chest of drawers, attempting to grab an improvised weapon from its top. She knocked the alarm clock, sending it crashing to the deck, before she seized the handle of her hairbrush. Camb easily dodged her attempt to hit his head. Instead, its hard bristles scraped down the back of his neck. He tore the hairbrush from her hand, throwing it to the floor.

Desperately, Gay flung her arm her out and behind her again, her fingers crawled up the wall to the bell-pushes and hit them for dear life, as long as she could. He lunged at her arm like a snarling grizzly, easily tearing it away, but he knew all too well that she had pressed them long enough to raise the alarm on the deck below. A visceral, incandescent rage consumed him, his anger distilling into pure malice.

He violently shoved her head back. In a flash, his right hand grabbed her throat. As his hold tightened ferociously, Gay felt the cartilage and sinews in her neck crush like a paper cup. The pain was incredible. Her eyes felt like they would explode. Gasping, she repeatedly clawed at his forearm with her left hand, digging her nails deep into his flesh, trying to drag his hand away. Her mind seemed to be disembodied, spinning in another dimension outside of reality. Then there was nothing.

Her grip on his forearm eased, her right fell to the deck like a broken branch. Her body went into spasm, twitching. Even when all movement had ceased, Camb kept his stranglehold, squeezing out the last hope of life until her body went limp. Her right eye was almost completely shut. The other was wide open and bloodshot. The skin around her open mouth appeared blue. As he released his grip, there was a faint gurgling from her throat. Bubbles of muddy-coloured saliva flecked with blood lined her lips. There were angry marks and bruises stippled with blood on her neck. Camb stepped back and took a breath. The receding rage was replaced by panic: Oh God, what had he done?

3:01am On the deck below, James Murray popped his head round the pantry door to see nightwatchman Frederick Steer lounging in his chair, feet on the desk, reading a magazine. "Did you hear the bells ring a few minutes ago?"

"Yeah," replied Steer, yawning. "I expect that old gal wants escorting to the toilet."

"And when are you thinking of going?" Murray asked testily.

Steer turned a page. "In a minute, I'm just finishing…"

"Go now!"

Sighing, Steer tossed his magazine onto the table and sauntered into the adjacent first-class dining room, whistling a tune. He shuffled up the steps, turned right and looked at the indicator board on the wall. When he saw both the red and green lights illuminated, he stopped whistling and hurried along the portside corridor.

3:02am There was a tap at the door. In disbelief, Camb turned to see it opening. Forcing it shut violently with the palm of his left hand, he bolted it. "All right," he called out.

"Damn!" he muttered under his breath. Had the nightwatchman recognised him? He could not be sure but how could he take the chance? When Gay's body was discovered, it would be obvious how she had died. And even if he had not been recognised, with his reputation for darting in and out of the cabins of female passengers, he would be the prime suspect. He knew no amount of smooth talking would get him out of this.

He stood motionless in the room, thinking. But what if she were never found? Without a body, no one would ever know what had happened. She could have fallen overboard after one drink too many. Even if he were suspected of involvement, he would flatly deny it. And there, just above the bed, was a perfect place to dispose of a body without it ever being discovered. He leapt on the bed. Straddling the body, he dragged it towards him, and heaved it into a sitting position against the outside wall under the open porthole. As he stood by the porthole, a faint breeze diffused into the cabin and he could hear gushing water from the bilge pumps below. Grabbing the body at the waist, he offered it up to the opening like a ritual sacrifice.

*

Members of the Cold Case Jury, there is one unassailable fact common to both reconstructions: James Camb was in Gay's cabin when the bells were rung. The prosecution's case, shown in the reconstruction you have just read, was that Camb observed Gay pushing the buttons and flew into a murderous rage of retribution. Yet, Joshua Casswell was convinced his client had been unaware that the nightwatchman had been summoned:

"If Gay Gibson had rung and Camb knew it, he had only to step outside and press the bulbs by the door to put out the indicator lights throughout the ship... Again, is it not abundantly clear that if Camb knew that Gay had rung the bells he would, in sheer prudence at least, have bolted the door and turned off the light? As soon as he did know – when Steer pushed open the door – he immediately slammed the door and bolted it."

In fact, Camb did not even have to step outside to extinguish the indicator lights – he could have reached them by opening the cabin door slightly and outstretching an arm. Bolting the door was easier still. The cabin was so compact that, even in the grisly act of strangulation, he could comfortably stand by the side of the bed, stretch out his left hand and slide the door bolt across. Even closer was the bedside light. With the cabin bolted, in darkness and silent, the nightwatchman would probably have tried the door, called out and then departed, thinking the call was a false alarm. But if Camb was consumed by a murderous rage, and entirely focused on his victim, could he have simply forgotten to bolt the door? This is for you to judge. But, for murder to be credible, there needs to be an explanation as to why Camb did not take such simple precautions to evade discovery before the nightwatchman arrived.

A curious feature of Camb's testimony was that he claimed Gay's alarm clock was left in the bar that night. There appears no reason to doubt this; it is surely too strange a detail for someone to invent. But why would Gay take the alarm clock from her cabin in the first place? Some have suggested that she wanted to send a symbolic message to Camb – now was the time, perhaps the hands signalling the hour for a rendezvous. If so, Gay was actively encouraging the deck steward to come to her cabin later that night. But is this plausible?

After his arrest, Camb told the police that on several occasions he had seen Gay alone on the deck late at night and "once when she passed me she had a clock in her hand". This might have been the night of her death, but it could also have been a different night altogether. If she had taken the clock with her more than once, this would suggest there was no special reason to be carrying it on the night she died. Indeed, there is a more prosaic explanation: she needed the clock for time-keeping because her wristwatch had broken, or she did not even own one.

In *The Porthole Case*, a chapter of his book *A Reasonable Doubt*

(1960), Julian Symons was sceptical about whether Camb had sufficient time to strangle Gay before the arrival of the nightwatchman. At the trial, expert opinion suggested that it takes approximately one minute for a victim to die from strangulation. Some current sources state that pressure must be applied for two minutes to cause death. As the nightwatchman Steer testified that he reached the cabin in no more than a minute, Symons believed that, if guilty of murder, Camb would have been caught in the act of strangulation when the cabin door opened.

By assuming a clockwork world, in which witnesses have a precise awareness of time, Symons makes a classic mistake of the armchair detective. How can we be sure that Steer reached the cabin in a minute? In fact, Steer previously stated, at the committal hearing in November 1947, that he took three or four minutes {see *Exhibit 9*}. He changed his mind after a marine surveyor testified that it was possible to reach the cabin within 30 seconds, or just over a minute at normal walking pace. When challenged about this inconsistency, Steer claimed that he "did not take any particular notice of the time" until later. Had Steer realised his job might be in jeopardy if he testified it had taken him so long to respond to the call?

Both of Steer's timing statements can be reconciled if he delayed his departure from A Deck by two or three minutes after the bells rang, instead of leaving immediately. Indeed, his boss Murray said he instructed Steer to leave, suggesting the nightwatchman had not left straightaway. A delayed departure was assumed in the reconstruction, giving Camb three or four minutes before the cabin door opened. This was plenty of time to have strangled his victim and stand beside the bed wondering what he should do next. Even if Steer did arrive promptly, it is possible that Camb stopped strangling Gay after a minute and stepped back. If Gay was not dead at this point, a crushed windpipe would ensure death soon followed.

There is a third explanation for the death of Gay Gibson:

manslaughter. If it is reasonable to believe that having sex in the stifling hot cabin caused sudden natural death, it is equally credible to suggest the stress and exertion of fending off an attacker led to the same tragic result. In this scenario, Camb's sexual assault resulted in the death of the actress, but there was no intent to kill. He would still have been motivated to dispose of the deadly evidence against him, especially if Gay sustained injuries during the assault. It also explains both his persistent lies and claims of innocence. He could not admit the truth without incriminating himself, and to admit manslaughter would end his freedom, career and marriage. The life he knew, and loved, would be over.

The case for manslaughter assumes Camb was unaware the nightwatchman had been summoned. How might the bells have been rung without his knowing? In his 1959 article for the *Sunday Pictorial*, Camb claimed he pressed the bells accidentally when he switched on the main cabin light {see *Exhibit 13*}, yet the switch was nowhere near the bedside panel. Even a dozen years after the event, Camb could not adequately explain how the bells rang.

One possibility is that while Camb was lying face down on top of Gay, she outstretched her right arm, perhaps to grab an improvised weapon from the chest of drawers, and her hand pressed against the bell-pushes. Or perhaps she pressed them to summon help. Even if Camb realised that Gay had reached for something, he might not have been aware the buttons had been pressed. Later, he would have figured out what happened, but was trapped by the truth. That would explain why he never offered a credible account of how the bells were rung. Admitting Gay died during a sexual assault would not persuade anyone of his innocence; it would be the quickest way to invite a murder charge and guilty verdict.

The biggest obstacle to accepting the manslaughter theory is the timing of the bells ringing and Gay's death. If Steer left for the cabin directly on hearing the bells ring on A Deck, it would mean that

Gay's very last act before she suddenly collapsed was to hit the bell-pushes. It is possible, but sounds more like a convenient plot device from a crime novel. But as we know, it is unclear how long Steer actually took to answer the call. The longer he dilly-dallied, the more credible the manslaughter theory – Gay might have hit the bell-pushes and then died during the exertion and stress of a prolonged assault.

Members of the Cold Case Jury, there are three possible verdicts: misadventure, murder and manslaughter. Based on all the evidence, which account is the most likely? To help us reach a decision, you will soon read never-before published documents from the police files. How they were unearthed, and the light they shed on the case, provide a remarkable final twist to our story.

Chapter 11

EVIDENCE UNSEEN

November 2015. One overcast afternoon, Paul Stickler, vice-chair of the Hampshire Constabulary History Society and former chief superintendent, receives a telephone call. Hampshire Constabulary is disposing of unwanted archived files. Would the society be interested in some paperwork concerning an old murder case? Paul affirms it is and retrieves two unassuming box files, saving them from incineration.

By sheer coincidence – or perhaps fate – I happened to call the society the very next day to enquire whether it had any information concerning the Camb case I was researching. Astounded at the timing, Paul generously allowed me to become the first researcher to inspect the police files. For a criminologist interested in the case, opening the boxes was like revealing Tutankhamun's tomb. The hundreds of yellowed pages, which I sifted and sorted over many months, contained the full trial transcript and the complete police record, including witness statements, detective reports, personal correspondence between Gay and her friends and family, photographs and even some numbered court exhibits.

I discovered that Southampton detectives had taken statements from nearly 40 witnesses, many of whom never testified at the trial. Buried in battered boxes and lost in time, their voices have been muted until now. You, the Cold Case Jury, are the first to hear them. How they alter the complexion of the case, if at all, is entirely for you to decide.

Some of the most interesting statements were provided by colleagues who worked with Gay Gibson during the ATS production of *Jane Steps Out* in the second half of 1946. The play had five major female roles, of which Gay played one. The four other girls in the play became acquainted with her, two of them closely. All gave statements to the police concerning Gay's character and conduct.

Mary Costerton joined Stars in Battledress two weeks before Gay, but the two did not become friendly until both were cast in *Jane Steps Out* in August 1946. She said Gay had "an idiosyncrasy that was outstanding, in that she would discuss herself with anyone, male or female, if they cared to listen. She always seemed to be out to impress and to invite criticism of herself as regards her acting, her conversation, her appearance and knowledge. This was so pronounced we used to tease her about it." Was it so pronounced that she would also have intimate conversations with a deck steward she had only just met?

Mary remembered Gay crying in the lounge of a Chester hotel when they were on tour. "This was not the outcome of any hysteria," she informed the police. "She was a person who could cry at will, and loved to dramatise herself. I don't know why she liked to do that but I suppose it was to attract attention to herself... She was not what I would call a neurotic person, although she had the makings of one. She would wake up in the night crying but that was always because she was cold."

She continued: "Gay was keen on singing but had to give it up because she had a weak chest. She used to catch cold very easily and cough a lot but hoped that when she went to South Africa her health would improve so she could take it up again... She used to feel the cold a lot and occasionally fainted when she was very cold."

Although the two did not discuss sexual matters, Gay "gave the impression that she was rather highly sexed". Nevertheless, as the pair worked so closely at this time, it would have been "impossible for Gay to have an affair" without her knowing.

Rosalind Thompson said that she was not particularly friendly with Gay. "She was so egotistical... She loved to dramatise herself and always seemed to think that her emotions were of the greatest interest to everyone else... she was very talkative and emotional. She could cry at the slightest provocation." She summed up her general character: "Gay was not what I would call neurotic, although she was highly strung and excitable." Her description is consistent with the view of Mike Abel and Henry Gilbert.

As to Gay's health, she confirmed that Gay did not like the cold. "I know she fainted about three times when it was very cold... her hands and arms would be blue with the cold" but she did not remember any illnesses that Gay had while they knew each other.

As regarding more personal matters, Rosalind stated, "Gay was what I regarded as highly sexed. She often talked about sexual matters and said she was 'repressed'. I know that Gay had an affair with a Frenchman during her first tour. His name was Pierre and she said she had been engaged to him and she had broken it off.

"She struck me as the sort of woman who would lead a man on to almost the limit and then refuse his sexual satisfaction. I have no concrete proof of this but it's my firm conviction. If she was really fond of a man, however, I think she would have slept with him because she was so keen on sex."

Rosalind also remembered that "Gay had an affair with a friend of her best friend's husband and they went out together as a foursome." We should not infer that any of these affairs involved physical intimacy. At that time 'an affair' often referred to nothing more than a few casual dates. Nevertheless, this remark is consistent with a pattern running through many of the statements: Gay seems to have attracted and welcomed the company of men. There are references to at least half a dozen 'affairs' or 'infatuations'.

Pat Rawlings, who joined the ATS in April 1939, confirmed that Rosalind and Gay "got on each other's nerves". By contrast, Pat became extremely friendly with Gay, discussing "almost every subject under the sun. We discussed sex very intimately. She was not very interested, and she struck me as having good morals... I do not know if she masturbated – I wouldn't like to give an opinion on that – but we certainly discussed that subject on occasions. During the last tour of *Jane Steps Out* Gay had an affair with one of the male cast members, but I don't think there was anything improper in the association."

She described Gay as "highly strung and very excitable" and confirmed Gay was self-absorbed, saying that on one occasion "we went to bed and lay awake talking to 3 o'clock in the morning. I remember this because it was one of the few occasions when Gay had had a long conversation without talking about herself." As regards Gay's health, Pat said it was normal except when the weather was exceptionally cold. "Then she went blue and fainted."

Pat remembered one occasion when she had a conversation with Gay's mother, who said she wanted her daughter "to leave the stage" and that "Gay had a weak chest". Daisy mentioned neither fact at the trial. Gay visited Pat in London before leaving for South Africa. "We had a few drinks and something to eat in the West End. She sailed the next day." She received three letters from Gay while she was in South Africa.

Jean Harding, the youngest of the four colleagues, knew Gay the longest, but it was not a close friendship. Jean said Gay was "a bit temperamental" but she was not hysterical or always crying. She was "the serious type" and liked to read Russian authors such as Tolstoy and Dostoevsky, but was rather gullible. She confirmed that Gay had a weak chest and wanted to work in a warmer climate.

"She used to feel the cold terribly and I have known her to faint with cold." She also added, "Gay would discuss sex at times but did not strike me as highly sexed."

The four statements provide greater insight into the health and character of Gay Gibson than was explored at the trial. None said that Gay was unhealthy, but it is clear she had a propensity to faint and for her hands and arms to turn blue, especially in cold weather. It should be remembered that Gay was in Johannesburg during winter when night-time temperatures can be low, even dropping to freezing occasionally. In fact, in a letter to her mother, Gay mentioned it was "extremely cold at night".

Gay fainted at least five times in Johannesburg, possibly more. Even if she was in the very early stages of pregnancy, this does not account for her fainting, as the same occurred in England the year before, and possibly earlier. We also learn that she suffered from a "weak chest" and one of the reasons for Gay travelling to South Africa was to improve her health. Doreen Mantle, Mike Abel and other members of the *Golden Boy* cast witnessed Gay fainting during rehearsals, when the skin around her mouth turned bluish. They also observed that "she had not been strong and were worried about her being able to carry on". Both Henry Gilbert and his wife Ena Schoub remembered Gay tiring easily.

What condition could account for these symptoms? Intolerance to the cold is a symptom of hypothyroidism, in which insufficient hormone is produced by the thyroid gland. However, this condition has other symptoms that Gay did not have, including lethargy, muscle pain, mental slowness and a puffy face. Recent research suggests abnormal levels of the thyroid hormone elevates the risk of sudden cardiac death but, if untreated, this condition typically drags on for years and leads to a slow, debilitating demise. Hypothyroidism is therefore unlikely, especially as its characteristic symptoms would have been noticeable and should have been picked up during Gay's army medical.

Raynaud's Syndrome is a condition where the smaller blood vessels that supply oxygenated blood to the skin go into spasm, trapping the blood so it deoxygenates causing numbness and cyanosis, a blue discolouration of the skin. These symptoms occur during periods of cold or stress, and are typically observed in the fingers. They can affect other parts of the body, but almost always the extremities, such as toes, nose, ears and lips. This would account for Gay's hands, lips and fingernails turning blue, but not her arms. More importantly, it does not explain her fainting, which is caused by a lack of oxygen to the brain and is not a symptom of Raynaud's.

Taken together, Gay's symptoms are consistent with congenital heart disease – fainting and cyanosis would occur because blood is not pumped fast enough around the body, causing it to deoxygenate. It would also account for her breathlessness and tiring easily. Interestingly, Gay was worried her "heart was affected" and she had "heart trouble". However, if she suffered from congenital heart disease, telltale signs should have been exhibited earlier and one would have expected it to be discovered during her army medical.

Having spoken to several medical experts, I found there is no way to be sure what condition Gay suffered from. I will return to this issue in the summing-up, but I think there is one conclusion we can safely draw. In terms of health, Gay Gibson was not "one of the finest types of English womanhood".

What did her friends say about her character? It is clear that Gay was egocentric and her main topic of conversation was herself, even to strangers, but even though Gay sought attention and loved to dramatise herself, none of her friends said she fabricated stories. This bears on the question of whether she told Camb she might be pregnant.

The day after the news broke of Gay's disappearance, a former Polish airman wrote to Southampton police. Wiktor Zorra met Gay in London during the spring of 1946 and the two became friendly for a while. His portrait of Gay is arguably one of the most insightful:

"She was well-read but education appeared to have been sketchy. Philosophy, ethics and psychology were invariable subjects of conversation, and she insisted on my imparting to her what little I knew of these things. She had recently read *War and Peace* and was deeply impressed by the character of Pierre Bezukhov, whose Hamlet-style instability made her think she had found in him a kindred soul. This, I believe, is no unimportant pointer to her character. She was always searching for a new faith, for the orthodox belief which she had lost left a disturbing void. She was unstable, not sure of herself, more often sad than cheerful. The plays we frequented in the West End made her reflect that she might never attain the fame she hankered after."

What about the crucial question of Gay's sexual behaviour? Had Rosalind Thompson stated in court her view about Gay's attitude to men, it would have been explosive. It suggested a possible motive for murder: Camb was led on by Gay only to be turned down on her bed. However, she also believed Gay would sleep with a man if she really liked him. Thompson offered much opinion but little fact on these matters, but this does not mean her view is inaccurate. Friends, as well as foes, can give distorted pictures of someone they know.

Gay told others she was sexually experienced, but was this merely the talk of a young woman trying to project a more sophisticated persona? Overall, her friends said Gay was interested in sex but doubted she was sexually active, let alone promiscuous. However, this was before her time in South Africa. The purchase of a contraceptive reveals that Gay was almost certainly sexually active by the time she left for England.

In the file there is a receipt for the diaphragm and contraceptive jelly found in her suitcase. They were purchased by Gay the day before she flew to Cape Town to board the *Durban Castle*. Like much surrounding the circumstances of her departure, it appears a last-minute decision. She consulted Dr Pollecoff, who later wrote to the police. From her conversations with Gay, the doctor believed she was cheerful, in good health and anxious to get back to England to complete her dramatic training. She would only say Gay had consulted her on a "private matter" – clearly patient confidentiality prevented her from divulging further information. Based on her discussions, however, she did not believe the rumours that Gay was promiscuous.

The file also contains copies of six letters to Gay from her parents. They were written while Gay was travelling home and were waiting for her in England, unread. They reveal a loving and close-knit family. Daisy was anxious that Gay was travelling home alone with no proper place to stay and no one to meet her, confirming that the departure was relatively sudden. From one letter, it appears that Gay had only recently decided to settle back in England – suggesting her return was initially temporary. If Hopwood and Bray were correct, the decision was far from final.

Charles Schwentafsky is mentioned in several letters and Daisy enquired whether he had written, anxious to know anything he said. Charles was hoping to build a factory in Durban and appears to have promised jobs to Gay's brothers and father. An obvious concern in the letters was Gay's health, although this was about keeping warm in the cold and wet of an English winter. Her father reminded her that she was "a hot house plant" while her mother wrote about rugs and blankets and injections for colds. Again, Gay's sensitivity to the cold is clearly apparent.

Daisy gave three of Gay's letters to the police. One was the last letter the family received from her, written on the *Durban Castle* five days before she died {see *Exhibit 10*}. Two were written when Gay first arrived in Johannesburg. Unfortunately, they tell us little. There is no record of the many letters Gay would have written during late summer when she was involved with *Golden Boy*, which would have provided far greater insight into the events leading up to her departure from the show and South Africa.

The police files did not only contain evidence concerning Gay – there were also revelations about James Camb. After his conviction was upheld by the Court of Appeal, a Sunday newspaper described three incidents in which Camb had assaulted young women on board the *Durban Castle*. Two had occurred on the outbound voyage to Durban and one on the trip from Durban to Cape Town before Gay boarded. Denis Herbstein suggested that the women probably came forward seeking publicity when the news of Camb's arrest became known. However, the women were said to have made affidavits to the South African police, and this is not the typical action of publicity-seekers, who tend to go straight to the newspapers. Fortunately, the affidavits were filed in the police records and add detail to what we know about Camb.

Three signed and sworn statements were made by different women in South Africa on 5 November 1947. Someone called Du Pooy, the police commissioner, forwarded them to Southampton CID. They were not used at the trial because Camb's character and past conduct were not at issue. As Joshua Casswell pointed out in his closing speech, the defence never argued that Camb was a man of unblemished character, and introducing his past conduct would have been prejudicial – the jury had to decide his guilt based solely on the evidence of the case before them.

These allegations are important, however, because they throw light on Camb's behaviour leading up to the death of Gay Gibson. They have never been published before. The relevant passages from the affidavits are reproduced in *Exhibit 11*. The three young women were aged between 16 and 19 years, and although no official complaint was logged, it certainly appears other members of the crew knew about the propensity of the deck steward to sexually harass young women.

Two incidents (Affidavits B and C) were similar. In both, a female passenger was sleeping alone in a cabin located in the same area of the ship as Gay would later occupy. Camb went uninvited to the young woman's cabin, made unwanted advances, and left. In both incidents the cabin was unlocked and Camb entered without locking the door after him. In one incident, he sat on the girl's bed and kissed her three or four times. In the other, he lay on top of the girl, kissed her face and pressed her breasts. In each case, the girl told him to stop and, eventually, he did. Both victims were shaken and frightened by the experience, but reported no bodily harm or violence.

The assault described in Affidavit A shows markedly different behaviour. Camb met the woman late one night in an equipment room on Promenade Deck. He brought drinks and locked the door behind him. When the woman asked to leave, Camb violently placed his hands around the woman's neck. After the attack, the victim returned to her cabin, distressed and with bloodshot eyes.

The most violent attack of the three occurred first. Did the deck steward tone down his aggression after this incident? Or was it just a matter of time before his violence erupted again? It should be noted that the brutality described in the first affidavit is the only recorded instance of violence by Camb in his life.

Although the affidavits were given only after Camb was arrested, two of the three were corroborated by another passenger {see *Exhibit 11*}. These statements indicate that Camb was a sexual predator who might turn violent. You may view them as damning evidence, although a more nuanced point should be considered. In both cases when Camb intruded into the cabin of a female passenger on B Deck and left the door unbolted, he inflicted no bodily harm. If this is what happened in Gay Gibson's cabin, it would be consistent with the manslaughter theory.

The more serious attack occurred when the young woman

agreed to meet Camb for drinks on his territory – a storeroom on Promenade Deck. Camb bolted the door behind him, possibly indicating that he believed she was willing to become intimate. When she refused, he allegedly exploded with rage. If this is a better indicator of what happened in cabin 126, it would be consistent with a verdict of murder.

Alternatively, because the veracity of these accounts was never examined in court, you might think they have little bearing on the case, especially if you believe other evidence suggests Gay welcomed and consented to Camb's advances. This view would be consistent with misadventure.

The police files reveal a wealth of information that formed the factual foundation of all the reconstructions you have read, allowing the story to be told in high definition for the first time. But would the battered box files give up any secrets concerning one of the most enduring and memorable features of the case – the mystery of the missing black pyjamas?

Chapter 12

THE DENTIST'S PYJAMAS

The trial, and the shocking events it revealed aboard the *Durban Castle*, sparked conversation and gossip, fuelled largely by lurid stories in tabloid newspapers. Indeed, there were few at the time in Britain who had not heard of the Porthole Murder and held an opinion on Camb's reprieve from the gallows. In pubs, factories and offices people dissected the case and discussed the rights and wrongs of the death penalty. One such conversation came to the attention of the police. In May 1948, three weeks after Camb's death sentence was commuted, a 34-year-old accountant walked into Cheltenham police station and told officers that he had information regarding one of the most sensational aspects of the case – the missing black pyjamas.

This accountant was already known to Gloucestershire Police. In a typed, single-page report, titled "The Murder of Gay Gibson" {see *Exhibit 12*}, they informed colleagues at Southampton that, although he was rational and well-educated, he "was thought to be suffering from some slight mental disorder". No details of his alleged psychological condition were offered, although the report stated that he had been bound over for stealing property from his lodgings and was suspected of stealing a bicycle. Perhaps mild kleptomania was the justification for the assessment, but the rider implied his claims did not deserve further investigation. As this police report is not in the public domain and unsubstantiated allegations were made about his mental health, I have decided not to name the accountant.

Detective Sergeant Quinlan received the report but appears to have made no further enquiries. This is not surprising. After all, the missing pyjamas were not a major plank of the prosecution case, despite the amount of column inches they generated in the tabloid press, and the information had a dubious source, at least according to the report. The form was date stamped, signed by Quinlan and filed. There it remained, hidden for decades, like an artefact lost in the deep.

When I received the box files from the Hampshire Constabulary History Society, I stumbled upon the report, tatty and torn and buried at the bottom of one of the boxes. I was intrigued by its claim, because it was consistent with that salacious rumour at the time of the trial: the black pyjamas were in the cabin of a distinguished passenger. Would this evidence reveal that Camb had told the truth all along?

Based on the police report, let us rewind time to 8:30pm on 17 May 1948. The place is central Peterborough, eastern England.

*

The man, dressed in a grey flannel suit, reached the corner of Broadway and Westgate. He discarded his cigarette by the base of a metal street lamp on which a set of traffic lights rhythmically flashed its sequence of colours. A little further along Westgate, a three-storey building rose above the roofs of the surrounding shops. On one side of its top storey was a large advertisement painted onto the brick facade – Bull Hotel.

Even at his languid pace, the man soon reached the sandstone facade of the hotel and entered. A stout man standing behind the long wooden bar nodded a welcome. "A Watney's brown ale," the customer ordered, looking around the sparsely filled lounge. There were a dozen people gathered at several tables, quietly chatting, and a couple huddled by a blackened fireplace, forlorn and disused now summer was almost here. Sitting at the bar was a smartly dressed man in his mid-20s, his jacket laid neatly over an adjacent stool. He was hunched over a newspaper reading the racing results in the sports section. A glass of whisky kept him company.

"That's one-and-three," the barman said, placing a bottle of ale on a Watney's beer mat.

"The price has gone up again!"

"Yep, and no stronger neither," the barman replied sympathetically. "This stuff ain't nothin' compared to the ale before the Great War. It were a man's beer then. Everything's changed, and not for the better, that's for sure." He placed a thick, dirty-looking glass before the customer, who completed the transaction by placing the exact change on the bar.

The customer sipped his beer and made eye contact with the sports fan, who outstretched his hand. "How do you do? My name's Langham, John Langham." The two shook hands. "So what brings you here?"

"This is my local, or it will be, I should say," the customer replied. "I'm moving here in a fortnight; on the 29th to be exact. I've got a place on Broadway."

"Can't say I know the place, old chap. I'm here on business."

"Oh, and what's that?"

"BBC."

"Really? Are you a reporter?"

"More research. Well, at least for the time being," Langham replied. "Have you heard of *The Progress Report*?"

"Can't say I have."

"It's on the Home Service. It's a survey – and this is a quote – a survey of Britain's production effort." They both laughed. "The last programme in the series aired the week before last. We visited a new steel works in Wales, a hydroelectric plant in Scotland and examined how new machines are improving worker productivity. I cannot imagine who would want to listen to such tosh." He sipped his whisky. "Apart from accountants, of course."

"I'm an accountant."

Langham was unfazed. "Sorry, old chap. No offence intended."

"None taken."

"I want to cover something that people care about, like sport or politics. Look what's going on at the moment with the death penalty." He prodded his newspaper with his finger. "That's something that matters."

"What do you think of the recent vote in the Commons?" the accountant asked.

"I agree with its suspension. In fact, I hope it leads to the abolition of capital punishment once and for all."

The accountant shook his head. "I think it's a big mistake. The ultimate crime deserves the ultimate punishment, doesn't it? It seems only right to me."

Langham took another sip of his drink. "I'm not so sure. Does the state ever have the right to kill its own citizens? Surely, it's compassionate, basic human decency to give someone the chance to atone."

"That's a prison reformer's myth! How many criminals even want to reform? You wait. This suspension will not change anything, except throw away the ultimate deterrent for crime. The sooner they bring it back the better."

"Well, if it's a deterrent then we should see an increase in capital offences while it's suspended, shouldn't we? If there's not, it proves it's no deterrent. And if it's no deterrent, why have it?"

"Justice, of course! An eye for eye."

"But if it's wrong for someone to commit a crime then surely it's wrong for the state to commit it too. Take murder. If it's wrong to kill a person, it's wrong, and that includes the state. This seems to be an incontrovertible point of logic, don't you think?" Langham smiled.

"Well, I see only one wrong and that's the murder itself. We're happy enough to take a life, millions of them, in a war for the sake of the country. Why can't we take a life for the sake of society during the peace? That's the way I see it. The vote to suspend the death penalty is plain wrong. It's already spared the life of that cold-blooded burglar."

"The one who shot the policeman?"

"That's right, the army deserter. Thomas something?"

"Donald Thomas, I think."

"He even went for his gun to shoot the arresting officers. What did he say? 'I might as well hang for a sheep as a lamb.'" The accountant picked up his ale and took several large gulps. "He deserves to get his neck wrung, all right. Society's a better place without him. Same goes for that Porthole Murderer. He's been reprieved too after breaking into that poor girl's cabin, raping her and dumping her body in shark-infested waters to cover up what he did. It's terrible."

"I could tell you something about that case!" There was a sparkle in Langham's eye.

"What do you mean?"

"I was told something about it last week."

"Oh?"

"You're not going to believe this! I saw my dentist last Wednesday. I have a problem with my jaw." Langham pointed to his face. "He's one of the best dental surgeons, apparently. He has a plush surgery in Cavendish Square. Anyway, as I was putting on my jacket to leave, we made some small talk and he mentioned that he was on the same voyage as the actress who disappeared."

"Did he see her?"

"He got an eyeful, all right!" He beckoned the accountant closer and lowered his voice. "He said he had a cabin next to hers. She was a flirty thing and on the night before the murder she came to his cabin."

"So the rumours were true!"

"Yeah, and he told that me after they had been properly introduced, so to speak, she left her black pyjamas on his cabin floor. That's why she wasn't wearing any when the steward came for his bit later on!"

"What did you say?"

"I said to him, 'Oh, come on, you're pulling my leg!' This is the unbelievable part. He walks over to a cabinet and opens the bottom drawer. And guess what he pulls out?"

"No!"

"Oh yes! A pair of black pyjamas! He unfurled them right in front of me. He said, 'Do you think I'm pulling your leg now!' I was stunned. Then I said, 'That's important evidence, why didn't you go to the police?' He said he couldn't risk the damage to his professional reputation, especially as the whereabouts of the pyjamas would have made no difference to the verdict. I said, 'But a man's freedom is at stake.' Had the reprieve not come through he would have contacted the police, or so he said, but there was no need now. The steward deserved a prison sentence for what he did, and he wasn't getting involved. With that, he folded the pyjamas and put them away."

"Blimey! I don't believe it! What are you going to do? You should inform the police."

"No, I promised I would not. And he's right, it makes no difference, except the papers would go wild with the story. He fears he would have to give up his career in London and leave the country if it gets out."

The accountant nodded. "Guess that's understandable. Well, it looks like you've made some progress in the case!"

"Yeah, but it's not something I can put in *The Progress Report*!" The two men laughed. The young researcher downed his whisky. "I need to get going, I'm afraid." He scooped up his jacket from the stool. "Nice talking to you. By the way, I would appreciate it if you could keep our little progress report to yourself." He winked.

"Of course," lied the accountant with a smile. He knew precisely who he was going to tell as soon as he returned to Gloucestershire at the end of the week.

*

Members of the Cold Case Jury, if there was ever an example of hearsay, this is it. The police received a third-hand story, one ripe for rumour and misinformation. There is so much scope for mistruth and exaggeration it is not surprising that it was not investigated. Did the conversation at the hotel bar actually take place, or was it an attention-seeking fantasy of the accountant? Did the dentist merely mention that he had been on the same voyage as Gay Gibson and the rest was barroom bravado on the part of John Langham? And even if Langham gave an accurate account, was the dentist merely grandstanding with his customers?

In his statement, the accountant did not provide the name of Langham's dentist, but this is hardly suspicious. As it was not material to the story, Langham probably did not mention it. Nevertheless, I was deeply sceptical of the whole episode. There were several letters in the police files from attention-seekers and confessors, and this looked like another example. Indeed, I suspected it was a yarn dreamt up by an accountant with a mischievous sense of humour. After all, the alleged conversation took place at the Bull.

I decided to investigate further. I started with the venue. Was there a Bull Hotel in Peterborough in 1948? This was easy to establish: yes, and it is still there today. The place was genuine, but what of the story? Could it be confirmed by either of the men involved? The accountant, who was in his mid-30s at the time of the conversation, was dead. What about the young researcher, John Langham? He rose through the ranks of the BBC, becoming a well-known presenter in the 1960s. He read the news and announced the classified results on *Grandstand*, the flagship sports programme for the BBC at the time. He was described as a charismatic man, who drove a Bentley, owned two restaurants and dated a string of beautiful women. One of his establishments was the Bistro Monte Carlo in Chelsea, a sports bar and restaurant, which attracted many BBC celebrities on its opening night. Tragically, Langham took his own life in December 1965 by jumping out of a window at Lime Grove Studios. He was 40 years old.

Although the accountant's tale could not be confirmed by either participant, there was another approach. If the story was false, it should be easy to disprove. If I could show there was no male dentist travelling first class on the *Durban Castle* with Gay Gibson, there could be no amorous liaison between a dentist and the actress, and the story would fall at the first hurdle.

A ship's immigration record, signed by the captain, lists every passenger, including name, age and occupation, arriving at a home port. I examined the one for the *Durban Castle* for that fateful voyage in October 1947. The typed record lists 250 passengers, of which 60 were travelling first class. I traced my finger down the column of names in first class, scanning each row for the stated occupation. On the first page were several company directors, housewives, an artist, a wool buyer, but no dentist. I noted that three entries were crossed off – the passengers who disembarked at Madeira. One was William Bray.

I continued my search on the second page. Poignantly, there was a line through the entry for Eileen Gibson. As my finger continued its course toward the bottom of the page I was increasingly confident that my suspicion about the conversation was correct. To my amazement, however, near the end of the first-class passenger list, a dental surgeon was listed. He was South African. I scribbled down his name on my note pad: Max Wolman.

This was a surprise, but I remained confident it was a coincidence. For the allegation to have any truth the dentist had to be travelling alone and quite young. If he was 70 years old or travelling with his wife, the chances of a young woman's pyjamas ending up in his cabin were remote. The data recorded in each row of the manifest included the passenger's age. The dentist was 43, old enough to find youth extremely attractive, yet young enough to possibly arouse the interest of a 21-year-old woman. Was he accompanied by a wife? No, he was listed in the manifest as travelling alone.

My hope of disproving the story was dashed. The accountant's statement could not be rejected as pure fabrication, at least not yet. In fact, the opposite was true. The facts provided a modest degree of corroboration. Another aspect was troubling me. If I were to invent such a story, I would choose a different profession for a cabin Lothario: a passionate actor, a dashing army captain, or a wealthy businessman. This gives a greater dramatic context, allowing listeners to be drawn into the tale – after all, most people are credulous and want to believe a good story. But a dental surgeon? Was this another small pointer to the truth of the incident?

Despite the facts I had unearthed, I could not rule out the possibility of coincidence. The presence of a middle-aged dentist travelling alone was to be expected if a stream of similar passengers was flowing from South Africa at the time. This could be checked. I randomly selected eight other voyages with a similar profile – Union Castle liners with a first-class service travelling from Cape Town to Southampton in 1947. I examined the immigration record of each one to see how many dentists were among those on board. Out of a total of 900 first-class passengers, I found only two other dentists. One was female. The other was married and travelling with his wife.

From this large sample, the only man of the right occupation, age and marital status was on the voyage with Gay Gibson. What were the odds of a coincidence now?

Ever sceptical, I thought of how I could further test the story. According to Langham, his dentist worked in Cavendish Square. If Max Wolman returned to South Africa soon after he arrived, or settled in a different part of the country, this would immediately discredit the whole account. So, where was Wolman working in early 1948? To answer this, I scoured the electoral rolls and discovered that, in April 1948, he was living at an address on Oxford Street, London. His apartment was less than 200 yards from Cavendish Square. The possibility of a coincidence looked even less likely. Wolman stayed in England for nearly 20 years, returning to South Africa in 1965, and died six years later.

Caution is required, however. Wild rumours often contain a kernel of truth. We cannot possibly infer from these facts that the entire story is true. Even if the accountant's description of the conversation is accurate, it does not follow that Langham or his dentist told the whole truth. Indeed, we cannot even be sure that Max Wolman was Langham's dentist. We can place him on the voyage and he was living very close to where Langham's dentist worked. Nevertheless, my failed attempts at refuting the story provide a degree of corroboration for it.

How else could I test the story? According to the report, the dentist occupied an adjacent cabin to Gay. Unfortunately, the immigration record does not list the cabin numbers of the passengers, but we know from the ship's plan {see *Exhibit A*} that three cabins shared the same alleyway as cabin 126, close enough to be described as adjacent. Cabin 124 was occupied by 74-year-old Henrietta Stephens. According to Eileen Field, Cabins 128 and 130 were not occupied by a female passenger because she would have attended to them. She also thought them unlikely to be occupied by a male passenger because she had not seen anyone near the cabins during the entire voyage. The steward, Reginald Boothby, made no mention in his police statement of anyone occupying these cabins. Given that the captain and the police interviewed Henrietta Stephens, it is unlikely they would have failed to take a statement from a male passenger in Cabin 128 or 130.

There was one other detail buried in the report. The alleged sexual encounter between the dentist and the actress occurred the night before her death, presumably a reference to the Thursday night. If the story is true, the pyjamas would have been missing on the Friday morning, but Eileen Field testified she was unable to find them on the Saturday {also see *Exhibit 5*}. If they had been missing for two days, surely she would have mentioned this important fact? She did not, and this casts further doubt on the veracity of the story.

Other than her dining companions Hopwood and Bray, there are no witness reports of Gay spending time in the company of another man during the voyage. On the other hand, we know from the two cups on the tea tray that Gay might have taken tea with someone in her cabin one night. Who was it? And why did they remain silent about the fact?

The discovery of the accountant's report only deepened the mystery of the missing black pyjamas, but the police files contained a final, tantalising clue about what might have happened in cabin 126.

Chapter 13

BY A HAIR'S BREADTH

July 2017. My mobile phone rings, the screen shows a withheld number. I hesitate. These are sometimes nuisance calls and normally I let them pass to voice mail. The caller will leave a message if it's important. Uncharacteristically, I swipe the screen.

"Is that Antony M. Brown?" The male voice is mellifluous.

"Yes."

"This is Richard Latto from the BBC." The name is unfamiliar, but I hope he is calling for an interview – my first book, *The Green Bicycle Mystery*, has just been published. "Are you the author of *Death of an Actress*?"

I am surprised. I self-published the progenitor to the book you are reading as a much shorter digital edition over a year earlier. Richard explains he wants to produce a programme to commemorate the 70th anniversary of Gay Gibson's death and the subsequent trial. We start talking.

I inform him we could do more than retell the story. I have the police files containing new evidence and exhibits from the trial.

"What exhibits?" he asks excitedly. "The porthole?"

"No, it was reconstructed for the trial by Harland and Wolff, and later returned to them. It's now lost, almost certainly destroyed." I look down. On my desk there is a green Invigorator hairbrush tagged "Exhibit 20. Rex v Camb." Gay's auburn hair is still clinging to the stiff bristles. A puff of air gently moves some of the strands; they tremble as if alive. Like a votive object, it provides an intimate connection to her.

"No, the most significant is Gay's hairbrush. It was one of her personal possessions recovered from the cabin by the police."

"Why is it significant?"

"I'm wondering if it is possible to extract DNA from her hair," I reply. "This might reveal whether she had a genetic predisposition to any of the health conditions mentioned at the trial. If she did, it would strengthen considerably the case for sudden natural death".

*

And so began our collaboration on a BBC documentary of the case. We were both keen to pursue the DNA story, but was it feasible to extract DNA from 70-year-old hair? If it was, would it provide the answers we wanted? And there was an ethical issue. Even if it was technically possible, was it morally right to proceed?

DNA is the complex chemical carrying the genetic code that determines the characteristics of every living thing, including humans. The complete genetic code of an individual is called a genome. Whole genome sequencing, as its name suggests, is when the complete DNA sequence of an individual is analysed, revealing all the genetic information about that person, including susceptibility to disease.

There are two types of DNA in a typical cell – one is found in the nucleus and the other in the mitochondria. Nuclear DNA contains the genetic code of the individual, and in humans determines virtually every characteristic from height to eye colour. Mitochondrial DNA contains much less information, mostly genetic code for the energy production of the cell. As an analogy, think of a highly complex device like a smartphone. If nuclear DNA is the blueprint for building the entire phone, including the circuitry, the screen, the camera and the physical case, then mitochondrial DNA is the specification of the battery. Its design is less complex, and by examining the battery you cannot figure out anything significant about the phone.

To discover more about the DNA in the strands of Gay's hair, we approached several experts. Mitotyping Technologies is a leading DNA-typing company based in the United States, which specialises in developing DNA profiles from hair strands. Gloria Dimick, a forensic DNA analyst at the company, immediately informed us it would not be as straightforward as we imagined. "Hair samples taken from a hairbrush are typically naturally shed hair, a hair shaft without the follicle," she explained. "This means you can only extract mitochondrial DNA, and this will not contain the genetic information you seek."

We needed samples of Gay's hair with the follicle attached, the only structure in hair that contains nuclear DNA. This is typically obtained when hair is pulled sharply from the scalp, perhaps during a fight or when taken intentionally as a sample. Our quest was further complicated because Gay's hair was 70 years old.

"It would be unlikely that nuclear DNA could be extracted from a hair sample of that age," Gloria told us. "As you know, with the passage of time, there is a natural degradation process in which the DNA starts to break down. In some criminal cases, our laboratory is sent hair samples that have degraded DNA – the hair might have been exposed to high temperatures and high humidity – and it is only possible to extract mitochondrial DNA because there are far more copies of it in a cell than nuclear DNA."

This was a blow. Even if some of Gay's hair in the hairbrush had follicles attached, the nuclear DNA was likely to have degraded. There were further complications. There might be other people's DNA on the hairbrush, from the skin cells of people who handled it, for example. This posed a risk of DNA contamination. According to

Gloria, if nuclear DNA was found on the hairbrush, it was more likely to be a modern contaminate.

And the problems did not end there. Even if we had usable nuclear DNA from Gay's hair, we would need to sequence the entire genome, and test for all possible genetic predispositions for sudden death. This is very different to the widely used DNA profiling in criminal and paternity cases, in which only a sample of DNA is used. Further, at the present time, there is no comprehensive genetic catalogue of risk factors for sudden natural death, whether from cardiac problems or other medical conditions. We were advised to postpone any DNA analysis until whole genome sequencing became more affordable and the genetic risk factors for sudden natural death are better understood.

We are not talking a delay of months, but years. We had to put the genetic testing of Gay's hair on hold. The Hampshire Constabulary History Society, guardian of the exhibits, has informed us they will seek to preserve the hairbrush in conditions that will arrest any further DNA degradation. Like a valuable piece of art, it needs a dry and stable environment. This means, as genetic technology and knowledge develop in the years to come, others might be able to investigate the genetic secrets kept by the strands of Gay's hair.

The hairbrush that Gay left behind on the chest of drawers was a trivial item that received little attention at the time. The secrets of DNA were not discovered by Francis Crick and James Watson until 1953, and no one could foresee how genetic technology would transform criminology as well as medicine. In the future, could her hairbrush reveal what happened in the past? It would be a fitting denouement to the case, and to her memory.

Richard Latto's documentary about the death of Gay Gibson is in production. It is due to be aired on the 70th anniversary of James Camb's conviction and death sentence. None of the court exhibits has ever been filmed before, so at the end of October 2017 I took them to the BBC studios in Southampton. As the hairbrush sat on a table in a sound studio, illuminated by bright lights and high-definition cameras, we noticed its black bristles were exceptionally hard and sharp like needles. "I wouldn't want to brush my hair with that!" Richard joked. "They're like cat's claws!"

Too stunned to respond, I recalled the medical report made by Dr Anthony Griffiths on board the *Durban Castle*: the injuries he observed on the back of Camb's neck were fine and "similar to those inflicted by cat's claws." Dr Griffiths was never handed the Invigorator hairbrush and asked whether it could have caused these scratches. Had he answered "yes", the most likely explanation is that there was a struggle in cabin 126, with Gay using the hairbrush as an improvised weapon.

Does the hairbrush, rather than the hair, provide the final clue as to what really happened to Gay Gibson?

Chapter 14

SUMMING UP

Members of the Cold Case Jury, one of the grounds for Camb's unsuccessful appeal against his guilty verdict was that Mr Justice Hilbery had not defined murder for the jury. In the view of the appeal judges, a definition was unnecessary – if the prosecution was right, and Gay Gibson was unlawfully killed, there was no case for the charge being reduced to manslaughter. It is true that James Camb was never going to admit that his attentions were unwelcome and Gay died during a sexual assault, but this is a possible scenario for you to consider. It is one of three potential verdicts:

Misadventure. Gay Gibson died suddenly while having consensual sex with James Camb.

Murder. Gay Gibson was strangled by James Camb when his advances were rebuffed.

Manslaughter. Gay Gibson died suddenly during a sexual assault by James Camb.

I suggest there are six pieces of key evidence that will determine your verdict. The first concerns **the cabin door**. How did Camb enter cabin 126 when Gay always bolted her door at night? Casswell suggested she must have known what he was after at that time and, by admitting him, she was amenable to his advances. And, once inside, why did Camb not bolt the cabin door to prevent his discovery? Even if he failed to lock it on first entering Gay's cabin, he could have easily stretched out his left hand at any time and flicked the bolt across. According to the misadventure theory, Camb did not need to bolt the door because there was no violence. He locked it when he realised his only option to save his life at sea was to dispose of the body.

Second, **Camb's injuries**. Why were there no scratch marks on Camb's hands? Scratches on the hands, and particularly the ball of the thumb, are arguably a more reliable pointer to strangulation than the release of urine, which sometimes occurs with natural death. Consider a simpler explanation: there were no scratches on Camb's hands because he did not strangle her. Instead, Gay clutched at him during her natural death throes.

What about the fine scratches on the back of Camb's neck? Dr Anthony Griffiths, the ship's surgeon, stated they "were similar to those inflicted by cat's claws". Gay's Invigorator hairbrush was an exhibit at the trial and yet he was never asked whether the hairbrush, with its hard, sharp bristles, was consistent with these injuries. If it was, it is possible that Gay grabbed a weapon to fend off the unwanted advances of the deck steward, and the cases for murder and manslaughter are strengthened.

Third, **the ringing bells**. Who rang both bells and why? The stark and indisputable fact is that Camb was in Gay's cabin when both buttons were pressed, but he consistently maintained that he had no idea how it happened. The explanation that he accidentally leaned against them was propounded by his lawyer in his closing speech, but was denied indirectly by Camb in the 1959 *Sunday Pictorial* articles. If Gay died naturally in the cramped cabin, is it plausible that Camb did not know how the buttons were pushed? The prosecution's case for murder assumed that he knew all too well: Gay pressed them to raise the alarm, and he silenced her.

But would Camb really strangle Gay if he knew the nightwatchman had been summoned? If he feared being caught in the cabin, surely he would have bolted the door to prevent his discovery? The alternative is that, unnoticed, Gay pressed the bell-pushes. It is possible Gay flung her right arm out in a moment of passion, yet Camb insisted it was around his neck. Did Gay inadvertently hit the buttons with the back of her hand while she was grabbing a weapon to fend off his unwelcome advances? If this were the case, and even if he knew how the buttons had been pressed, Camb could never admit this without conceding he was forcing himself on the actress.

Fourth, **the missing pyjamas**. Where were Gay's black pyjamas? To accept the misadventure theory, you must assume it was a dreadful coincidence that the pyjamas went missing on the night Gay Gibson died, never to be found. The case for murder, by contrast, has an explanation: they were underneath her dressing gown. Camb never realised she was wearing them, and he fabricated the story about Gay being naked to indicate that she was anticipating intimacy with him.

But does the accountant's conversation suggest Camb was telling the truth? Despite doubts over two details, the truth of its central allegation cannot be disproved. Yet, if it were true, and the pyjamas were in the dentist's possession, why did nobody else come forward over the years to confirm the story? Would the dentist have told only a BBC researcher?

Fifth, **the disposal of the body**. Why did Camb push Gay's dead body through the porthole? If he murdered her, he could not leave the body on the bed with its damning evidence of strangulation. Even if he fled the scene unnoticed, he would have been the prime suspect given his reputation. His best option to avoid being charged with a capital offence was to dispose of the "deadliest evidence" of his guilt and deny that he was ever in her cabin that night. If Gay died naturally, he had other, arguably better, options: if there was time, fleeing the cabin would have been a more instinctive response.

Even after the nightwatchman tapped on the door, he had the opportunity of facing the consequences then and there.

An advocate of misadventure might counter that Camb's reputation left him with little choice but to dispose of the body, especially if he believed he might have been identified by the nightwatchman. This was something he could not admit at his trial without opening up the issue of his previous conduct. And his conduct was far from exemplary. Although not tested in court, the affidavits of the three young women allegedly assaulted by Camb must be given due consideration. The more weight they are given, the more the balance of evidence tips away from misadventure.

The sixth and final point is **Gay's health.** If you believe Gay had a serious health condition that could cause sudden death, this increases the likelihood of misadventure or manslaughter. If you think otherwise, the case for murder strengthens considerably.

Professor James Webster believed that Gay's chronic ear infection might have caused toxic myocarditis, a potentially fatal heart problem. Her army medical recommended she should not be stationed in a tropical climate on account of the infection, but merely passing through on board the *Durban Castle* should not have been a problem. This was confirmed by the officer who performed the medical. Further, Gay never complained about her ear to her friends, or in her letters home.

We know that in South Africa Gay tired easily and had "a weak chest", yet these were not symptoms her friends remembered when she was in England. Without doubt, Gay was intolerant to cold weather when her hands, fingernails and lips turned blue. This is consistent with Raynaud's Syndrome, but fainting is not. It should be remembered that Gay fainted in England as well as in South Africa; it was a pronounced symptom. If she suffered from Raynaud's, which is not a cause of sudden natural death, her fainting was caused by another, unrelated condition.

Gay's symptoms appear consistent with congenital heart disease, a potentially fatal condition that would be triggered not only by the cold but also physical and emotional stress. According to Doreen Mantle, Gay fainted in the theatre during rehearsals for *Golden Boy*, when it was not noticeably cold. She also stated that the cast were concerned that Gay looked unwell and fatigued, and might not be able to go on with the show. But if she suffered from a weak heart, would it not have been detected during her army medical? And how can the evidence of her English friends be reconciled? They said Gay appeared to be in good health most of the time only a year before, apart from her fainting in cold weather. Was her condition deteriorating?

Keeping all this in mind, it is now time to turn to the evidence. In Act Two, you will find maps, plans, photographs, witness statements and background information. None of the documents from the police files has ever been published before. These are not mere footnotes to the story. They allow us to see the crime scene, hear witnesses in their own words and place events in their full context. Only after seeing the original evidence will you be in a position to decide what really happened in cabin 126 on the *Durban Castle*. In Act Three, I provide my view of the case and the verdicts of other authors.

After examining the original evidence, I hope you will deliver your verdict. Visit the Cold Case Jury website (**coldcasejury.com**) and simply click on 'Your Verdict' for *Death of an Actress* and follow the simple instructions. After you have cast your vote, you can view the collective verdict of the Cold Case Jury.

It is now up to you, the jury, to decide how Gay Gibson died.

ACT TWO

The Evidence

Our story is not yet finished.
It can only be completed by listening
to the narrator of every crime.

The evidence.

List of Exhibits
PLANS AND DIAGRAMS

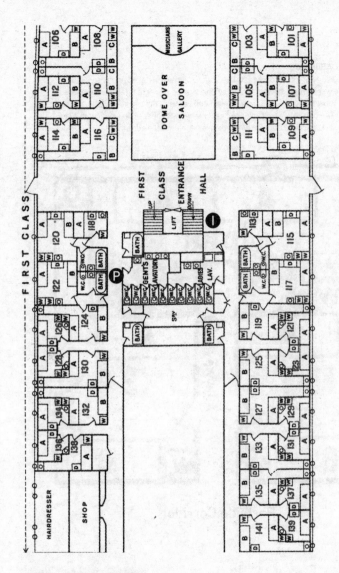

EXHIBIT A: SECTION OF B DECK

The first-class entrance hall was also known as "The Square". Gay Gibson occupied cabin 126 on the portside of the *Durban Castle*. Nightwatchman Fred Steer ascended the stairs (marked with a "down" arrow) from the deck below, and turned to his right to look at the indicator board (I). This told him both bells had been rung from a cabin on the portside of the deck. He would have proceeded to look for lights down the portside corridor (P). On the far wall of the alleyway, he saw the red and green lights illuminated for cabin 126.

EXHIBIT B: CABIN 126

Cabin 126 was one of four accessed from a shared alleyway. The red and green lights for cabin 126 were situated at the end of the alleyway, on the right (L). The door opened inwards, as shown. The bell-pushes were situated between the bed (A) and the chest of drawers (D). The porthole was above the bed. Henrietta Stephens occupied cabin 124. The other two (128 and 130) are believed to have been unoccupied.

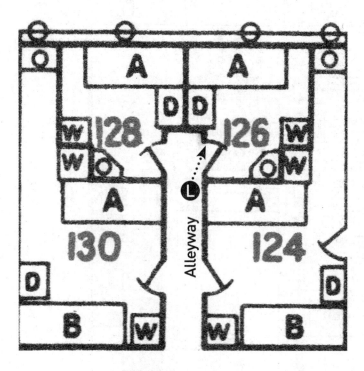

Portside Corridor

CABINS:
124 Henrietta Stephens
126 Gay Gibson
128 Unoccupied
130 Unoccupied

KEY:
A Bed
B Second bed
D Chest of drawers
W Wardrobe
O Washbasin
L Indicator lights (Cabin 126)

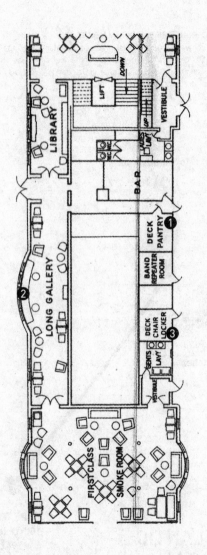

EXHIBIT C: SECTION OF D DECK
Also known as Promenade Deck, this was exclusively for the use of first-class passengers. Below the Smoke Room was the veranda, which overlooked the first-class swimming pool towards the stern (not shown). James Camb worked from the Deck Pantry (1) and first met Gay Gibson in the Long Gallery (2) on Saturday 11 October 1947. The Deck Chair Locker (3) was the scene of Camb's alleged violent attack {see Exhibit 11}.

EXHIBIT D: ROUTE OF THE *DURBAN CASTLE*
This map shows the route of the *Durban Castle* after it left Cape Town
on Friday 10 October 1947. The position of the liner when Gay's body was
thrown overboard at 3am on Saturday 18 October 1947 is indicated.

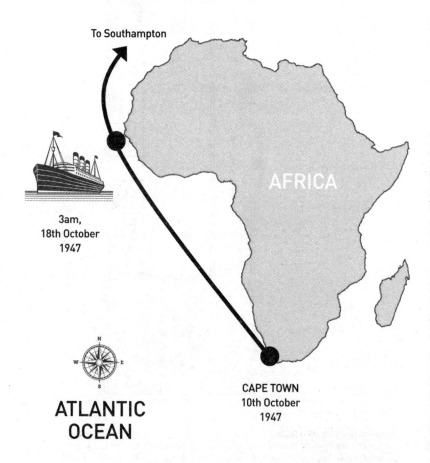

To Southampton

3am,
18th October
1947

AFRICA

ATLANTIC
OCEAN

CAPE TOWN
10th October
1947

EXHIBIT E: CAMB'S SIGNED STATEMENT

This is an image of the actual police statement signed by James Camb. It is stamped with Exhibit No. 24. The text of the statement was reproduced verbatim in Chapter 6.

Statement of James Camb.

I have been cautioned by Detective Sergeant Quinlan that I need not say anything and that anything that I do say will be taken down in writing and may be given in evidence.

Signed... *James Camb*.

I have already stated to you that I went to Miss Gibson's cabin at about eleven o'clock on Friday 17th October 1947 and during the course of conversation with her I made an appointment to meet her that night. I knocked at the door after I had finished work about one o'clock but there was no answer. I opened the door of her cabin and found that it was empty. I then went foward to the well-deck where I sat for about half an hour smoking. I then returned to Miss Gibson's cabin about two o'clock and found her there. After a short conversation I got into bed with her with her consent. Intimacy took place. Whilst in the act of sexual intercourse she suddenly clutched at me foaming at the mouth. I immediately ceased the act but she was very still, I felt for her heart beats but could not find any, she was at this time very still, and I cannot offer any explanation as to how the bells came to be rung as I most definately did not touch them myself. Thinking she had fainted I tried artifical respiration on her, whilst doing this the night watchman knocked at the door and attempted to open it. I shut the door again saying it was allright. Then I panicked as I thought he had gone to the bridge to report to the officer of the watch, as I did not want to be found in such compromising position. I bolted the door and again tried respiration. After a few minutes I could not find any sign of life. After a struggle with the limp body, by the way she was still wearing her dressing gown, I managed to lift her to the port hole and pushed her through. I am fairly certain that at the time she was dead but I was terribly frightened. I then went foward and turned in. The time would be about 3.30.AM. I have read this statement over myself and it is true.

Signed. *James Camb*

The above statement was typed by Detective Constable Plumley in the presence of Detective Sergeant Quinlan at Police Headquarters, Southampton commencing at 7.0.PM. and terminating at 7.30.PM. 25th. October 1947.

COUNTY BOROUGH OF SOUTHAMPTON.
25th October 1947
REX v. CAMB
EXHIBIT. No. 24.

EXHIBIT F: *SUNDAY PICTORIAL* ARTICLE

This front-page was published on 13 September 1959 to publicise the five-article series about "the truth" of what happened on the *Durban Castle* 12 years before. Professor James Webster believed Gay Gibson died from myocarditis caused by chronically poisoned tonsils, the evidence for which was never stated.

SUNDAY PICTORIAL

September 13, 1959 • • No. 2,317 Fourpence
THE NEWSPAPER FOR THE YOUNG IN HEART

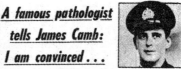

A famous pathologist tells James Camb:

I am convinced . . .

JAMES CAMB

PROFESSOR WEBSTER

YOU DID NOT KILL GAY GIBSON

I HAVE just witnessed the strange reunion of two men who last saw each other at a murder trial eleven years ago.

It was a dramatic meeting between—

JAMES CAMB, forty-two-year-old former ship's steward, who was sentenced to death—but later reprieved—at Winchester Assizes in March, 1948, for the murder of beautiful twenty-one-year-old actress Eileen (Gay) Gibson; and

PROFESSOR J. M. WEBSTER, the famous Home Office pathologist whose evidence has helped to send several murderers to the gallows.

Expert Says 'I Am Convinced'

And I heard the professor tell Camb: "I am convinced that you did not murder the girl."

Camb, released from Wakefield Jail, Yorks, last week at the end of his "life" sentence, met Professor Webster at a Birmingham hotel. They shook hands—and then sat down to discuss the trial that made legal history as "The Murder Trial Without a Body."

For Camb was accused of strangling Gay Gibson in her cabin aboard the liner Durban Castle on a voyage from South Africa, and then pushing her body through the cabin port-hole. Her body was never found.

Camb's story was that she died while they were making love and that it was fright and panic that made him get rid of the body.

Professor Webster was asked to give evidence for the Crown. He refused, and instead gave evidence for the defence at the trial.

And this week he told Camb: "On the evidence, which was disclosed, and, more particularly, on the evidence which was not disclosed, you might very well not have been convicted."

Speaking with the vigour of a cross-examining counsel, he went on:—

"Camb, I will not spare my words."

"Camb, if you died at the trial, then you were guilty."

Gay Gibson . . . her body was never found.

By HARRY ASHBROOK

Because I am convinced you did not murder the girl.

"There are still some questions which must be answered fully—but I have a scientific conviction that your story was the true one."

Then Professor Webster told Camb why he decided to give evidence for the defence and not the prosecution.

"In my experience I know of three cases where people died in the same way as Gay Gibson.

"And when I did see the evidence that was submitted to the jury my opinion about your version of what happened to her was confirmed."

Hour of Questions

For more than an hour Camb rapidly faced Professor Webster's barrage of questions about events in Cabin 126 on the night of October 18, 1947.

And afterwards, as he left Camb sitting alone, the professor told me: "I am more than ever convinced that he IS telling the truth."

What did Camb tell Professor Webster to convince him? What DID happen in Cabin 126? The full, dramatic story, in James Camb's own words, will soon be told in the Sunday Pictorial.

'If You Told Truth'

"Camb, if you told the truth, you should not have been found guilty of murder. But I do not think you told the whole story."

He paused, then added quietly: "I have lived with this problem for eleven years.

"It has never been out of my mind."

JAMES CAMB'S *own story will be published exclusively in the Sunday Pictorial soon*

Billy Butlin to wed

HOLIDAY camp king Billy Butlin announced yesterday that he is to marry the woman the world has known for years as Mrs. Norah Butlin.

They were unable to marry because a girl Billy married 32 years ago refused to give him a divorce.

She died last year.

And Billy has asked Pictorial columnist Rex North—on the left in the picture—to be the best man. SEE PAGE 14.

Billy and Norah Butlin yesterday—with best man Rex North on the left.

List of Exhibits
DOCUMENTS

Exhibit 1: Annual Timeline

The following timeline provides a wide-angled view of events connected to the death of Gay Gibson and the subsequent trial of James Camb.

1916
December 16: James Camb born at Waterfoot, Lancashire
1917
February 22: Edith Lillie Camb dies aged 39
1926
June 13: Eileen Isabella Ronnie Gibson (later known as Gay Gibson) born at Jamalpur, India
November 2: Joseph Gibson and family return from India to Birkenhead
1933
September 10: James Camb begins career at sea as a galley boy on the *Rotorua*
1938
June: Union Castle Line launches *Durban Castle*
1939
March: Joseph Gibson starts work in Persia (Iran)
September: James Camb joins Merchant Navy Reserve for his war service
1940
March: Gay and Daisy Gibson travel to Persia
1941
June: Gay and Daisy Gibson evacuated to India before returning to England
December: Gay appears in pantomime at Liverpool Empire
1943
September 11: James Camb marries Margaret Clark McCombie
1944
August: Gay starts training as a nurse at Waltham Hospital, Liverpool
1945
February 9: Gay Gibson joins Auxiliary Territorial Service (ATS)
November 15: James Camb released from Merchant Navy Reserve
1946
January: Gay Gibson joins Stars in Battledress, an entertainment troupe of services personnel
February: Gay in London rehearsing for the play *The Man with a Load of Mischief*
April: Tour of *Mischief* begins
April 9: James Camb joins crew of *Durban Castle* (assistant cook)

July: Gay Gibson has a fit and is treated by Evelyn Armour
August 3: *Mischief* tour ends
September: Gay in London rehearsing for *Jane Steps Out*
October 7: Tour of *Jane Steps Out* begins
November 2: Sid James and his wife arrive in Britain {see *Exhibit 14*}
November 26: James Camb joins crew of *Stirling Castle* (assistant steward)
December 11: Gay has alleged fit in Wales
December 17: *Jane Steps Out* tour ends
1947
January 9: Camb joins crew of *Capetown Castle* (assistant steward)
January 31: Gay spends six days in hospital (ear infection)
February 19: Gay undergoes army medical for compassionate release from ATS
February 26: Gay and her mother leave for South Africa on the *Carnarvon Castle*
March 12: Gay and Daisy Gibson arrive in Cape Town and travel overland to Durban.
April: Gay relocates to Johannesburg
June 13: Gay appears in *The Silver Cord* and celebrates 21st birthday
June 27: Camb joins crew of *Durban Castle* (deck steward)
July: Gay given the part of Lorna Moon in *Golden Boy*
August: Rehearsals start for *Golden Boy*
September 8: Boxer Eric Boon loses fight to Giel de Roode in Johannesburg
September 10: *Golden Boy* opens at the Standard Theatre, Johannesburg, with Eric Boon as the lead
September 18: Camb allegedly attacks a young woman on the *Durban Castle* {see *Exhibit 11*}
September 20: Standard Theatre closes
September 21: Camb allegedly sexually assaults a young woman on the *Durban Castle*
September 22: Gay leaves *Golden Boy*
September 26: Gay and Charles Schwentafsky check into Torquay Hotel, Durban
September 30: Gay and Charles leave Torquay Hotel
October 1: Gay and her family inspect the *Durban Castle* while moored in Durban
October 3: *Durban Castle* leaves Durban
October 7: Camb allegedly sexually molests a young woman in the early morning; *Durban Castle* arrives in Cape Town
October 8: Gay Gibson flies to Cape Town from Durban
October 10: Gay Gibson boards *Durban Castle*, which leaves for Southampton

October 18: At approximately 3am, Gay Gibson disappears from *Durban Castle*

October 23: Union Castle notifies Southampton CID of the disappearance of Gay Gibson

October 24: *Durban Castle* arrives at Cowes Roads, Isle of Wight

October 25: Camb taken to Southampton police headquarters

October 26: James Camb charged with the murder of Gay Gibson

October 31: First reading of the Criminal Justice Bill in the House of Commons

November 5: South African police take affidavits from three women about Camb's behaviour {see *Exhibit 11*}

November 17: Committal hearing begins at Southampton Magistrates' Court

November 21: Sydney Silverman announces his intention to amend Criminal Justice Bill with a motion to suspend the death penalty for five years

November 24: Camb sent for trial

December 2: Original trial date – this is postponed to enable defence witnesses to travel from South Africa

December 12: Gibson family arrive at Southampton, pending trial

1948

March 18: Trial of James Camb opens at the Great Hall, Winchester

March 22: James Camb found guilty of Gay Gibson's murder and sentenced to death

March 26: Second reading of the Criminal Justice Bill in the House of Commons

April 13: Original execution date of James Camb (postponed due to appeal)

April 14: House of Commons passes amendment to Criminal Justice Bill, suspending death penalty for five years

April 16: Home Secretary announces suspension of death penalty

April 26: Camb's appeal dismissed by Court of Criminal Appeal

April 30: Home Secretary commutes James Camb's death sentence to life imprisonment

May 17: Alleged conversation at the Bull Hotel, Peterborough, about missing black pyjamas

May 21: An accountant informs police of the black pyjamas disclosure {see *Exhibit 12*}

June 2: House of Lords votes to remove death penalty suspension from Criminal Justice Bill

July 15: House of Commons passes a compromise bill restricting the death penalty for murder with "express malice"

July 20: House of Lords reject compromise bill

July 22: Death penalty clause dropped from Criminal Justice Bill

July 30: Criminal Justice Bill (without death penalty suspension) becomes law

November 18: Stanley Clark becomes the first convict to be hanged in nine months

December: Margaret Camb divorces James Camb on grounds of adultery

1957

March 21: Homicide Act, limiting the death penalty for murder, becomes law

1959

September 7: James Camb released from Wakefield prison after being "a star prisoner"

September 27: Camb's story serialised in the *Sunday Pictorial*

October 25: Last article in serialisation published

1962

March: Final voyage of the *Durban Castle*

1965

November 8: Death penalty for murder suspended for five years

1969

December 18: Death penalty for murder permanently abolished

1971

April 17: Joseph Gibson, Gay's father, dies.

May 28: James Clarke (formerly Camb) imprisoned for harassing schoolgirls

1978

September: James Clarke released from prison

1979

July 7: James Clarke dies of a heart attack

1986

March 8: Daisy Gibson, Gay's mother, dies

Exhibit 2: Hourly Timeline

The following timeline provides a close-up view of events on board the *Durban Castle*. An asterisk denotes events according to James Camb's testimony. Some times are estimates.

Friday 17 October 1947

20:00 Dinner dance commences on Promenade Deck, attended by Gay Gibson

23:00 Dinner dance ends; Gay Gibson in Smoke Room with dinner companions Frank Hopwood and William Bray

23:15 Gay goes to her cabin to find swimsuit; James Camb talks to her in the Long Gallery

23:20 Camb visits Gay's cabin and says he will join her later *

Saturday 18 October 1947

00:00 Gay on Promenade Deck, talking to Bray and Hopwood

00:30 Camb starts washing up in the Deck Pantry

00:40 Bill Pott talks to Camb in the Deck Pantry; on leaving he observes Gay talking to Bray and Hopwood on Promenade Deck

00:45 Hopwood accompanies Gay to her cabin on B Deck

01:00 Gay observed on Promenade Deck by William Conway; this is the last independent sighting of Gay Gibson

01:05 Camb hands alarm clock to Gay Gibson on Promenade Deck after finding it in the bar *

01:10 Camb finds cabin 126 empty *

01:15 Camb is on the Well Deck, smoking *

02:10 Camb returns to cabin 126 *

02:25 Sexual intercourse begins between Gay and Camb *

02:40 Gay Gibson dies; Camb tries to revive her *

02:58 Emergency bells ring in the A Deck pantry; nightwatchman Fred Steer goes to investigate

02:59 Steer arrives outside cabin 126 (according to Steer's committal testimony, he would have arrived at 03:02)

03:04 Steer and head nightwatchman James Murray arrive outside cabin 126

03:10 Murray informs second officer on bridge about incident; Steer commences nightly patrol

03:15 Camb ceases attempts to revive Gay and pushes her dead body through the porthole *

03:20 Murray returns to cabin 126, now in total darkness, and leaves

03:30 James Camb arrives back in his cabin and turns in *
09:57 Captain Arthur Patey informed that Gay Gibson is missing
10:20 *Durban Castle* reverses course
11:20 Patey questions Camb
11:40 *Durban Castle* resumes course
12:00 Patey seals cabin 126
Sunday 19 October 1947
11:45 Dr Anthony Griffiths, ship's surgeon, examines Camb

Saturday 25 October 1947
00:00 *Durban Castle* anchors at Cowes Roads, Isle of Wight
00:05 Detectives John Quinlan and Minden Plumley travel by tug and board the *Durban Castle*
01:15 Hopwood gives police statement
03:00 Steer gives police statement
04:00 Murray gives police statement
04:45 Detectives examine cabin 126
05:25 James Camb interviewed by detectives in the Smoke Room
06:20 *Durban Castle* docks at Southampton
06:30 Camb arrives at police headquarters
07:00 Police resume enquiries aboard the *Durban Castle*
08:15 Police take photographs of cabin 126
12:00 Stewardess Eileen Field gives police statement
12:15 Dr Griffiths gives police statement
14:00 Camb gives consent for his injuries to be photographed
17:15 Detectives Quinlan and Plumley interview Camb
18:30 Detective Sergeant Gibbons briefly joins interview
19:00 Camb agrees to give statement
19:30 Camb signs written statement
20:00 Plumley obtains Camb's permission for blood test;
Camb allegedly makes confession [1]

Sunday 26 October 1947
13:30 James Camb charged with the murder of Eileen 'Gay' Gibson

Notes: [1] The confession was almost certainly fabricated by Minden Plumley. I have ignored it.

Exhibit 3: The Captain's Log

The following entries reveal how the news of Gay's disappearance was handled by the captain and his senior crew. My comments are italicised in parentheses.

Date: 18 October 1947
Position: 11.34 N, 17.39 W (*off the coast of Guinea-Bissau*)

At 9:57am today the chief steward reported to the master that a first-class passenger from cabin 126 named Miss Eileen Gibson could not be found. She had failed to appear in the Dining Saloon for breakfast.

The master proceeded immediately to make inquiries to satisfy himself that an efficient search had been made and forthwith held an enquiry into the disappearance of this lady. This enquiry was held in the presence of the chief officer and the purser and the chief steward.

At 10:20am being satisfied that Miss Gibson was not on board the master gave orders for the ship's course to be reversed with the intention of carrying out a search. The following message broadcast throughout the ship:

A FIRST-CLASS LADY PASSENGER, MISS EILEEN GIBSON, CANNOT BE FOUND. ANY PERSON WHO KNOWS WHERE SHE IS, OR CAN GIVE ANY INFORMATION CONCERNING HER, PLEASE REPORT AT ONCE TO THE PURSER.

A radio urgency message was sent out to all ships:

FROM DURBAN CASTLE STOP MISSING ON BOARD BELIEVE LOST OVERBOARD ONE LADY PASSENGER BETWEEN 0400 GMT POSITION 09.55 N 16.22 W ON COURSE 323 AND 0900 GMT POSITION 11.19 N 17.27 W STOP WILL ALL SHIPS IN THE VINCINITY PLEASE KEEP A GOOD LOOKOUT.

(At 3am, the Durban Castle *was positioned at approximately 9.12 N 16.3 W – 200 miles off the coast of Guinea. See Exhibit D for map).*

The following persons were called and interviewed by the master: Mr F W Hopwood (first-class passenger); Squadron Leader W R Bray (first-class passenger); Mr W Conway (boatswain's mate); Mr F P Steer (nightwatchman); Miss E Field (stewardess); Mr J Camb (steward); Mr J Murray (head nightwatchman); Mr A M Thompson (second steward); and Mr A White (second officer).

At 11.40am after hearing the statements of the aforementioned persons, it was assumed that Miss Gibson disappeared at some time between 3am and 7:30am today: and that no reasonable hope could be entertained of recovering her by retracing ship's course any further. To confirm this assumption the ship's doctor was consulted and he agreed that no useful purpose could be served by continuing to search for her. The master then gave orders to resume the ship's normal course. Cabin 126 was then visited by the master accompanied by the chief officer and the purser and found to be in an immaculate condition *(having been tidied and cleaned)*. Nothing was touched or removed: then the cabin was locked and sealed to await any investigation.

At 12.30pm the following message was received from SS "Reventazon":

RE: YOURS 18TH: 1222 GMT MESSAGE. I AM COVERING THE ROUTE TO SEARCH.

Date: 19 October 1947
Position: 11.25 N, 17.27 W *(off the coast of Guinea-Bissau)*
The following statements were recorded during the master's enquiry this day.

Mr Hopwood of cabin 33 and Squadron Leader Bray of cabin 105 stated that they both accompanied Miss Eileen Gibson from Promenade Deck at about 0035 hours and left her outside cabin 126. She then appeared to be quite normal in every way.

Mr Conway, boatswain's mate, stated that he last saw Miss Gibson (a passenger with auburn hair, wearing black evening dress and silver shoes) on the port side of Promenade Deck, when the watch were washing down this deck at about 0100 hrs. He advised her to go across to the starboard side to avoid getting her feet wet. She, however, chose to disregard this advice.

Mr Steer, nightwatchman, reported that he first saw this lady at 0030 hours outside the Smoke Room on the portside of Promenade Deck with Hopwood and Bray. Later, at approximately 0300 hours, "red" and "green" bells started ringing insistently from cabin 126. Nightwatchman Steer attended at once to cabin 126, knocked on the door, tried to open it but the door was forced against him by a man dressed in navy blue trousers and singlet wearing a brown leather belt. Steer is of the opinion that this man resembled Deck Steward J Camb.

The man said something like "It's all right". Steer then called Head Nightwatchman Murray, who proceeded with Steer to cabin 126, and remained outside there for about five minutes, and although the light was still on inside the cabin there was no noise from inside. Murray then proceeded to the Bridge and reported to Mr White, the second officer, that the bells had been ringing from cabin 126, also that there was a man inside the cabin, and that Steer had been unable to open the door against the man inside.

Mr White asked Murray if everything was all right, to which Murray replied, "Yes." Mr White remarked that he could not interfere with passengers' morals. Murray then returned to the alleyway outside cabin 126 and, as he could not hear any sound from the cabin and seeing that the light had been put out, resumed his normal duties.

Mr J Camb, deck steward, on being informed by the master that a person resembling him was seen in cabin 126 at about 0300 hours today replied, "I was not in that cabin at that time, and I was not in any passenger accommodation or on passenger decks after 0045 hours, at which time I got to bed."

Miss E Field, stewardess, stated that she went to cabin 126 at 7:30am today in the usual way with orange juice, knocked at the door, tried the door handle, and found the door unfastened, which was unusual as the door had been bolted on all other mornings this voyage. Miss Gibson was not in the cabin when Miss Field entered, the bed was turned back, and appeared to have been used. She then went to ask the bathroom steward if Miss Gibson was in the bath, but he had not seen Miss Gibson today. About 7:50am Miss Field called at cabin 126, where the orange juice was untouched and concluded Miss Gibson was on deck. At 8:40am Miss Field asked the head waiter of the first-class dining saloon to inform her if Miss Gibson appeared for breakfast. At about 9:20am, hearing the lady had not appeared for breakfast, Miss Field asked several of the stewards in the public rooms if they had seen her. None had. Miss Field then looked around the decks herself and finally at 9:30am reported the absence of Miss Gibson to the second steward, Mr Thompson, who at once searched the passenger decks and accommodation and then reported, at 9:45am, to the chief steward.

Date: 20 October 1947
Position: 25.34 N, 17.20 W (*off the coast of Morocco*)
Three packages of personal effects were removed from the Baggage Room holding the property of Miss Eileen Gibson, the missing passenger, and transferred to a special cabin. Being locked and intact, they were taped, sealed and labelled for safekeeping. Packages as follows: one large cabin trunk, buff coloured; one leather suitcase, camel coloured; and one hatbox of brown leather. Key of cabin kept by purser.

Date: 21 October 1947

Position: 32.14 N, 16.56 W (*approaching Madeira*)

At 10:30am today, the following statement was made to the master by Steer, night watchman. "At 8:45am this morning I saw Deck Steward Camb in the forward wash house. He asked me if I had made the suggestion it was him *(in the cabin at 3am)*. I said, 'No.' He then said, 'Thank goodness. I haven't been with her this trip. It's put me in a tight spot.' He also told me he had a medical."

(*Despite the implication of the phrase "I haven't been with her this trip," records show that James Camb and Gay Gibson had never previously travelled on the same ship.*)

Exhibit 4: What the Nightwatchman Saw

This is the police statement of Fred Steer, the 39-year-old nightwatchman on the *Durban Castle*, who on three occasions was summoned to Miss Gibson's cabin. My comments are italicised in parentheses.

I remember at about 3am on the morning of 18 October 1947, I was in the First-Class Pantry (*on A Deck, immediately below B Deck*) when I heard some bells ringing. I immediately went up the stairs to the indicator on B Deck, and found that bells had been rung for both the steward and stewardess. It is unusual for both to be rung. As a result of examining the indicator, I established that a passenger required my attention in cabin 126 [1].

I then went to cabin 126 on B Deck, knocked on the door, without response. I therefore attempted to enter the room and opened the door slightly. A man's voice said, "All right." The light was on in the cabin. Standing near the washbasin in the cabin, I saw a man who I recognised as Mr Camb, a deck steward on board the ship.

I would describe him as follows: back hair, brown eyes, dressed in a white singlet with shoulder straps, a pair of blue or black trousers, brown leather belt. He was standing to the left of the door with his back to the mahogany locker (*chest of drawers*) and I had a view of his right side. The door was pushed shut and I was not allowed to enter the room. I saw the door pushed with Camb's right hand (*but it was Camb's left palm print that was found on the inside of the cabin door*).

I returned to the First-Class Pantry, where I saw Mr Murray. I told him the bells were ringing in cabin 126 and he returned to the cabin with me. I remained outside (*in the corridor*) while Mr Murray went to the cabin. He returned and told me that the lights were out and that everything was quiet. (*Although Murray stated that the cabin light was on at this time.*)

On Sunday 19 October at about 8:45am (*it was actually Tuesday 21 October*), I was in the forward wash house, in the steward's accommodation, when I was approached by Mr Camb. He said, "Do you suggest it was me?" I knew to what he was referring – the disappearance of Miss Gibson. I said, "No." I knew Camb had been to the captain and asked him who had said it was him in the cabin, and the captain had told me not to tell anyone about it. He then said, "Thank goodness. I have not been with her this voyage, homeward bound. I'm in a tight jam." He also stated that he had undergone a medical.

Four to five days after leaving Cape Town, between 10:30pm and 11pm, Miss Gibson rang her bell, which I answered. I saw Miss Gibson in her cabin. She was fully dressed. She asked me to ask the deck steward for her tray. I went to the Long Gallery where I saw Camb and asked him for Miss Gibson's tray. I accompanied him to the pantry where he prepared tea and sandwiches and handed me the tray. I took it to her cabin and noticed that there were two cups and saucers on it. I thought perhaps the other cup might have been for Mr Hopwood or Mr Bray. She took the tray from me at the door. I did not enter her cabin. I then resumed my usual duties.

A night or two afterwards I was again summoned to Miss Gibson's cabin, between 10:30pm and 11pm. She again asked me to ask the deck steward for her tray. On this occasion, she was wearing a dressing gown. I came to the pantry, saw Camb and told him that Miss Gibson wanted her tray. He came to the pantry with me but I prepared the tray. I took the tray to her cabin, knocked on the door, and the tray was taken by Miss Gibson. On neither of these occasions did I enter the cabin and I am unable to say whether any other person was with her.

From what I saw of Miss Gibson, I thought she was a very nice girl, a moderate drinker and not the type to encourage a member of the crew to her cabin.

Notes: [1] Steer asserted that the cabin number of the summoning passenger could be determined from the indicator board, but he was contradicted by the head nightwatchman, the ship's electrician and the captain.

Exhibit 5: What the Stewardess Did

Eileen Field was the 35-year-old stewardess who became acquainted with Gay during the first week of the voyage. This is her police statement, signed at midday on 25 October 1947 when the *Durban Castle* was moored at Southampton docks.

On Friday 10 October 1947 I left Cape Town on the *Durban Castle*. I had in my care all female passengers occupying cabins with even numbers on B Deck. One of the persons in my care was Miss Eileen Gibson, who was travelling alone to England. She informed me she hoped to make her way on the English Stage. She seemed very enthusiastic about her career.

The day of joining the ship she mentioned that she was very much in love with a married man. In my opinion, she was in no way unhappy regarding it. She appeared very pleasant, quiet and gave no bother whatsoever. She followed regular habits and most evenings was accompanied to her cabin by two men I know as Hopwood and Bray.

Two or three days previous to the disappearance of Miss Gibson, I had occasion to meet deck steward Camb in the pantry. I was returning a tea tray which Miss Gibson had used. I said, "Here is the tea tray from Miss Gibson." Camb replied, "Miss Gibson is three months pregnant by a married man." I formed the opinion this was not correct and said, "It is very wrong to go round saying things like that about a lady passenger." He then said, "Miss Gibson told me herself that this is so." From this remark, I concluded that Camb was on familiar terms with Miss Gibson, although he has made no other remark which would give me that opinion.

During the afternoon of 17 October 1947, I saw Camb in the Square of B Deck. He was standing with his hands on the rails and facing the main stairway. The steward Boothby came along while he was standing there. I said to Camb, "What are you doing here?" and he replied, "Miss Gibson hasn't had her afternoon tea tray." I said, "There's nothing in that. She probably didn't want it."

His general demeanour gave me the impression that he was very concerned that Miss Gibson had not had her afternoon tea. I said to him, "If I find you in the vicinity of Miss Gibson's cabin, I will report you to the chief steward." He then smiled and shortly afterwards left the Square. It is most unusual for a deck steward to be in the Square on B Deck. That is the reason I rebuked Camb for his presence.

I last saw Miss Gibson at 6:30pm on Friday 17 October 1947, apparently dressed for the evening dance, and she was in good spirits and cheerful.

At 6am the next morning, the nightwatchman Murray came to my cabin and informed me that he rather suspected that Camb had been in Miss Gibson's cabin during the night, when he investigated the ringing of the bells at 3:30am (*the discrepancy in timing was never clarified*). I informed him that I would keep a lookout to see if Camb entered the cabin.

At about 7:30am, I knocked on the door of cabin 126, without response, and upon trying the door found it unbolted, which was most unusual, as Miss Gibson always bolted her cabin door. I entered and found Miss Gibson was not there. The bed appeared as though someone had slept in it; it was a little more untidy than usual. I noticed a stain on the pillow case and also on the sheet. The porthole in the cabin was open, which is usual practice for Miss Gibson.

I made various enquiries as to the whereabouts of Miss Gibson, without result. I paid frequent visits to her cabin and did not find her there. I noticed that all her footwear was in the cabin. This was unusual as she never left the cabin without footwear. I knew that when she returned to bed at night she usually dressed in either a blue nightgown or black pyjamas. She also wore a yellow flowered dressing gown when leaving the cabin. The dressing gown was of a cotton material, the predominant colour being yellow. The morning following her disappearance I found the black pyjamas and dressing gown were missing, but the blue nightgown was folded at the foot of the bed.

One morning – I cannot remember the date – I found a tea tray containing two cups and saucers and a teapot, which had been used, in her cabin. I knew these articles came from the Deck Pantry. On three occasions I collected small spirit glasses from her cabin; they undoubtedly contained liquor.

The sheets on a bed in a passenger's cabin are usually changed once a week. I have never at any time seen stains of any kind on Miss Gibson's sheets or pillows, until the morning of 18 October 1947. I found bloodstains and other marks on her pillow and bottom sheet. This was most unusual as Miss Gibson's bedclothes were never soiled.

Before I reported Miss Gibson missing, I tidied up the cabin and noticed on a chair and on the bed the black stockings and brassiere, and on a hook at the bottom of the bed I noticed the black evening frock which she had worn the previous evening. About 11.55am 25 October 1947, I reconstructed Miss Gibson's cabin in the manner in which I found it on the morning of 18 October 1947.

Miss Gibson never complained to me of suffering from any illnesses or any heart complaint. She always appeared fit and well.

Exhibit 6: What the Companion Said

Frank Hopwood, 48 years old, was an official of the Union Castle
Line in South Africa. He was travelling on the *Durban Castle* to
holiday in England. He gave his police statement on board the liner
after it docked. My comments are italicised and in parentheses.

On Friday 10 October 1947, I embarked on the *Durban Castle* at
Cape Town en route to England. When the ship was about to leave
Cape Town I made the acquaintance of Wing Commander Bray
(*William Bray was actually a squadron leader*) and arranged that we
would both sit at the same table in the dining room during the
voyage. On the same day, at dinner time, I went to the dining room
with Bray and found sitting at our table a lady whom I now know to
be Miss Gibson. We became friendly and during the voyage had
frequent meetings.

During the time that I associated with Miss Gibson I had several
conversations with her, the main topic being her stage career – she
told me she acted under the name Gay Gibson and also appeared in
army shows in England. She further stated that she had been in
Germany. On several occasions during the course of our
conversations she mentioned she was in love with a man called
Charles, a married man whose wife was in England. She appeared
to be in some doubt as to whether she would remain in Africa to be
near Charles or return to England to continue her stage career. She
informed me that she had several letters of introduction to theatre
agents in this country and on one occasion showed me one of them.
She spoke of her parents residing in South Africa, and that she had
arrived with her mother about six months ago, travelling from
England on the *Carnarvon Castle*.

During the time I had known Miss Gibson on the ship I found her
to be a well-behaved girl, not an excessive drinker and, to the best
of my knowledge, she was of sound moral character. She was of a

quiet demeanour at times. On occasion, she stated that this was owing to the fact that she was unable to arrive at a decision about the action she should take regarding Charles. She did not partake in any deck games: she stated the reason for this was because she was suffering from heart trouble. She did not state what kind of heart trouble. On occasion, she showed me her fingernails which appeared to change from the normal colour to a muddy brown, which she stated was due to bad circulation.

During the evening of Friday 17 October 1947, with Bray, I had dinner with Miss Gibson, who appeared to be in a very jolly mood. Immediately after dinner, we went on the Promenade Deck, where a dance was in progress. During the evening I noticed that Miss Gibson had many dances with numerous persons. The interval, which lasted from 9:30pm to 10pm, came and Miss Gibson, Bray and I went to the Smoke Room for drinks. We remained there for a matter of two hours. About 11pm, Miss Gibson expressed the desire to go for a swim in the pool as she observed other passengers passing through the room for that purpose. She left the Smoke Room, stating that she was going to her cabin to get a swimsuit. The Smoke Room closed at 11:30pm that night, and Miss Gibson had not returned to our company by that time.

Shortly after 11:30pm, she returned and informed us she was unable to find her swimsuit and it might be in her baggage on the ship. At about 11:45pm we went on the Promenade Deck and remained near the ship's railings until after 12:30am. The three of us went off the deck together. We then went onto B Deck, where Miss Gibson's and Bray's cabins were both situated. Bray left us and went to his cabin. I took Miss Gibson to hers, put the light on, remained there a few minutes and, after wishing her 'goodnight', went to my cabin on C Deck. This had been my practice throughout the voyage from the time we left Cape Town and until her disappearance. When I left her in her cabin the night prior to her disappearance, she did not give any indication that she intended to leave it again.

At no time during my association with Miss Gibson did she give any indication that she intended to commit suicide or do any harm to herself. On no occasion during the voyage did I see her having a conversation with any member of the ship's company. Miss Gibson was quite normal. I did not notice anything unusual in her demeanour. She appeared quite healthy.

I have never, at any time, had tea in her cabin after 11:30pm at night (*this leaves the possibility that he had tea with Gay in her cabin before this time*).

Exhibit 7: What the Actress Remembered

Doreen Mantle is best known in the UK for her portrayal of Jean Warboys in the BBC sitcom *One Foot in the Grave*. She acted with Gay Gibson in *Golden Boy* at the Standard Theatre in 1947. Now 91-years-old, she is the only surviving member of the cast. Richard Latto of the BBC interviewed her in November 2017 for his documentary on the case. She was extremely articulate, with a clarity of thought and recall that would be the envy of someone 25 years younger. Below are key quotes collated from her 40-minute interview.

On *Golden Boy*

"The lead was played by a boxer, Eric Boon, who came out from London. He had never acted before. He did his best, but it was not a great performance. I think Henry Gilbert played the father, and he would have got a good notice. There was a beautiful girl called Gay Gibson, who had also come out to South Africa, although I don't think she intended to settle there. She played the heroine. I also remember Mike Abel."

On Gay's Character

"She was more sophisticated than me, and knew about the world. She had travelled and knew about being with important people. She was unconventional for those days. She had older boyfriends. She was very sweet, warm and kind. I think she flirted, as girls do. She was not the placid type, but I don't remember her making scenes. I liked her, but I like most people!"

On Gay's Appearance

"She was a lovely looking girl. She had good cheekbones, with rosy cheeks at times that turned pale when she wasn't well. She bit her nails, and this is something I remembered from the case because

James Camb had scratches, and I found that strange because she didn't have nails that could scratch."

On Gay's Health

"She was not a well girl. This is what I told the defence team when they came out to see me before the murder trial. She fainted sometimes at rehearsals. I knew she went blue around her mouth and her hands were bluish. Although I didn't know anything about medicine, other cast members said this was a heart condition. It was unusual and worrying, but she would not discuss it. I thought she had a weak heart. There were times when she felt she wasn't well, and her nails went blue."

On Gay's Relationships

"I didn't know her intimately. We shared a dressing room, and we were friendly but that's as far as it went. She shared make-up tips and little things. Apart from one party, I did not go out with the cast because I was working as a social worker during the day. At that party, I remember her having a big argument with Mike Abel, accusing him of making her pregnant, which was a big thing in those days. Nobody talked about these things. I was shocked."

On Gay's Death

"We all read that she had disappeared off the *Durban Castle*. One day I was in my tiny office when I was told there were two rather tall Englishmen who wanted to talk to me. They asked me to come to their office later that day and said they were from the defence on the Gay Gibson murder case.

"They asked a lot of questions. I told them about the party and Mike Abel, and I told them about her health, that she had not been strong and we were worried about her being able to carry on. I prefaced everything with 'I think she may have' because I had no evidence at all that she really had a poor heart. They said, 'That's wonderful. When you come to England, we will want you to give evidence for the defence.' I told my father, and he said, 'You're not going to London!'

"They wanted me to sign an affidavit which said she had a heart condition and was unhealthy. I said, I can only say what I saw and what I think. I got legal aid, and my lawyer said I would not be travelling to England. The letters from the defence team kept on coming, saying that my evidence might save James Camb's life, which was very emotive language to use.

"I was on holiday on the south coast of Natal when my brother phoned me and said the verdict had come through: it was murder. I was in a terrible state, but I don't think I would have helped. Mike Abel and Henry Gilbert saw the same things, and if they did not listen to them, why would they listen to me? The defence thought I would be believed because I was a social worker, had nothing to hide and various members of the cast were involved with her, but I wasn't. Awful things were said about Mike Abel and Henry Gilbert to destroy their characters in court."

Exhibit 8: Trial Minutes

The following summary provides a complete schedule of events at the trial and includes the key testimony of every witness. Note that unless stated otherwise, dates in the testimony refer to 1947 and times refer to the evening of Friday 17 October 1947 or the early hours of the following day. *My comments are italicised.*

THE TRIAL OF JAMES CAMB

Venue: The Great Hall, Winchester Castle, Winchester
Date: Thursday 18 March 1948
Duration: Four days
Judge: Mr Justice Malcolm Hilbery
Prisoner in the Dock: James Camb, 31 years old
Counsel for the Crown: Geoffrey Roberts, assisted by Mr Elam and Mr Clarke
Counsel for the Prisoner: Joshua Casswell, assisted by Mr Molony

First Day: Thursday 18 March 1948
Arraignment
The clerk of the assize read the indictment for murder on the high seas, and asked the defendant how he pleaded.
Camb: Not guilty.

The Case for the Crown
Geoffrey Roberts outlined the facts of the case and the reasons why the prosecution believed Camb was guilty of murder. Ultimately, it rested on the disposal of the body. If Gay Gibson had died a natural death, why would Camb have undertaken such physical effort to push it through the porthole when he could have slipped from the cabin unnoticed? Roberts claimed this was conclusive evidence against the defence claim of natural death.

Ernest Minett, police sergeant, stated that he took measurements of cabin 126. It was 8' 4" long, 8' 6" wide and 8' 5" high.

Arthur Patey, captain of the *Durban Castle*, told the court of the events of Saturday 18 October. The two notes written by James Camb to the captain were introduced as evidence. He confirmed that if Camb had been found in a passenger's cabin he would have been dismissed and finding a position with another shipping line would be difficult.

John Addis, detective constable, explained the photographs he took in cabin 126 and of Camb's injuries. He also confirmed that fibres from the brass ring on the edge of the porthole were removed for forensic analysis. Under cross-examination, he agreed that the bell-pushes projected outward and would ring if someone leaned against them.

Sidney Birch, detective chief inspector of New Scotland Yard, confirmed that the palmar impression found on the inside of the cabin door was identical to the left hand of the prisoner.

Percy Law, detective inspector of New Scotland Yard, stated he made the photographic exhibits of the palm prints {see photographic plates}.

Frank Hopwood, Union Castle Line official, stated that at times Gay Gibson was rather depressed or worried and appeared tired. Her wheezing was not noticeable but she did speak of taking injections. *The detail Hopwood provided in his police statement {see Exhibit 6} was not fully brought out in court. Although he also gave a statement to police, Squadron Leader Bray was not asked to testify.*

William Pott, steward, saw James Camb in the Deck Pantry at 12:45am on the night of the dinner dance. Shortly afterwards, he saw Gay Gibson, Hopwood and Bray standing on D Deck (Promenade Deck). He also remembered Camb wore a long-sleeved coat on Saturday 18 October but on no other day.

William Conway, boatswain's mate, talked briefly to Gay Gibson when she was on the portside of Promenade Deck at approximately 1am. There were no other passengers on deck at the time.

Frederick Steer, nightwatchman, recalled the events surrounding his summons to cabin 126 in the early hours of 18 October {for further details see *Exhibit 4*}. When the cabin door was forced shut, he immediately reported back to James Murray, his superior.

James Murray, senior nightwatchman, stated that at 2.58am the bells in the galley of A Deck rang for a second, or one-and-a-half seconds, and he instructed Steer to answer the call. Steer left and returned three or four minutes later. Murray then accompanied Steer to cabin 126, estimating that he arrived five minutes after the bells had rung. The cabin lights were on, but there was no noise from inside the cabin. Murray waited outside, listening, but heard nothing. Even though Steer had informed him that he saw Camb inside the cabin, Murray did not report this fact to the second officer because he did not want to land the deck steward in trouble. *Murray provides a precise time for the ringing of the bells, although it was never established how he knew this with such accuracy. Additionally, in his police statement he said the bells rang "continually" and Steer told the captain that they rang "insistently", suggesting the ringing lasted much longer than a second or two. This discrepancy was never cleared up.*

Eileen Field, stewardess, under questioning from both counsels,

gave most of the information she provided in her police statement
{see *Exhibit 5*}. She stated she had never known both bell-pushes to
have been pressed accidentally, although conceded it was possible.
At the committal hearing she stated that both bells had been rung
by accident in the past, although not often.

Frank Allen, electrician, had tested the bell-push circuit from cabin
126 and found no fault. He confirmed that the bells would ring for
as long as the buttons were pressed.

Helena Baker, Gay Gibson's cousin, stated she saw Gay two years
previously when she was in the ATS and was in good health.

Second Day: Friday 19 March 1948
The Case for the Crown (continued)

Dr Anthony Griffiths, ship's surgeon, examined James Camb on
Sunday 19 October. On the back of Camb's neck, there were six to
nine fine scratches that appeared to be have inflicted by something
like "cat's claws". These were unlikely to have been caused by the
rubbing of a harsh towel and were recently inflicted. On the left
shoulder were several superficial scratches, at least three days old.
There were also several superficial lesions on the left wrist, which
looked like scratched spots, most likely inflicted several days prior
to the examination. On the right forearm were nine to 12 scratches
that "went across the front of tendons and radiated obliquely
towards the thumb, running across the wrist". They were entirely
consistent with fingernails "gripping" the arm with "some movement
following".

*In his report, Dr Griffiths stated the fine scratches on Camb's neck were "not
parallel". In court, he stated the opposite; he most likely misremembered
this detail when he testified.*

John Quinlan, detective sergeant and senior investigating officer, gave an account of his interview with James Camb {see *Chapter 6*}.

Herbert Gibbons, detective sergeant, gave an account of his participation in the interview of James Camb {see *Chapter 6*}.

Minden Plumley, former detective constable, claimed Camb confessed to the murder of Gay Gibson. Witnessed only by the constable, the prisoner allegedly said, "I can't understand why the officer on watch didn't hear something. It was a hell of a splash when she hit the water. She struggled, I had my hands round her neck and when I was trying to pull them away, she scratched me. I panicked and threw her out of the porthole." Plumley denied leaking information to the *Sunday Chronicle*, which ran a story on the case on 26 October. He also denied his resignation from the force in January 1948 was due to unsatisfactory performance.
The alleged confession was ignored by the prosecution because it added no additional weight to their case and was almost certainly fabricated.

Walter Montgomery, senior scientific officer, analysed the items removed from cabin 126. The top pillow had tea stains; the bottom pillow traces of lipstick; the bottom sheet two small bloodstains; a hair found in the bed matched those of a hairbrush found in the cabin; and the fibres removed from the porthole were fragments of down feather similar to ones found in the two pillows. The blood on the sheet was not from James Camb – he was blood group A, the stains group O.

Phyl Macdonell, ATS medical officer, stated that there was no record of Gay Gibson receiving medical attention while she was in service.

Audrey Puttock, ATS lance corporal and medical orderly, confirmed she was present when Gay's medical was performed by Dr Haslam.

Dr Ruth Haslam, ATS medical practitioner, confirmed she conducted Gay's medical on 19 February 1947. She found scarring on the right eardrum from an ear infection, which had recently discharged, and her hearing was impaired. She also had slight bronchitis but nothing abnormal was discovered. Gay was discharged as "AW/1/Non-Tropical". So, the outcome of the medical was that her general condition was fit but a station in a tropical climate should be avoided on account of her ear condition. Dr Haslam also stated that Gay had her tonsils removed when she was 11 years old.

The last point is relevant given Professor Webster's later claim that Gay was suffering from chronically poisoned tonsils {see Chapter 9}.

Ellen "Daisy" Gibson, Gay's mother, gave a resolute defence of her daughter's health and character. Her daughter was very healthy and happy to be returning to England. She denied that Charles Schwentafsky was involved romantically with Gay, and stated that his huge monetary gift was a business loan. She was highly disparaging of Henry Gilbert and his associates {see *Chapter 7*}.

Dr Donald Teare, pathologist, thought blood-flecked saliva was consistent with strangulation. He refused to offer an opinion on the scratches on Camb's forearm based on a photograph taken eight days after the incident. He believed that if Gay suffered from poor circulation, he would expect other symptoms – breathlessness and attacks of blueness on the face and lips – in addition to blue fingernails. On cross-examination, Dr Teare was surprised to learn that urine had been found on the bed sheet which, in his opinion, increased the probability of strangulation {see *Chapter 7*}.

According to Doreen Mantle, the skin around Gay's mouth turned blue

when she was not feeling well. This was also confirmed by Mike Abel. All the
South African witnesses observed that Gay tired easily.

The Case for the Defence

Joshua Casswell opened the case for the defence in a relatively brief speech. He stated that the defence would call two expert witnesses. Dr Frederick Hocking's testimony would show that the physical evidence was consistent with someone dying from the result of asthma or some kind of heart failure. Professor James Webster's opinion was first sought by the Crown, but his testimony would show it was "very probable" that the woman died in the way the prisoner claimed. With such reasonable doubt, Casswell argued that the jury could not possibly convict in this case.

James Camb, the accused, gave his account of what happened (see *Chapter 8*). The most significant admission was his claim that Gay was naked underneath her dressing gown, a detail he did not mention in his police statement. He also stated how he tried to revive Gay, by first massaging her chest to bring back a heartbeat and then by artificial respiration. These attempts lasted 15 minutes, during which time nightwatchman Fred Steer knocked on the cabin door.

Third Day: Saturday 20 March 1948
The Case for the Defence (continued)

James Camb resumed his testimony, recalling his interview with the police. Apart from categorically denying Plumley's claims, he did not contradict the police account of what happened in the interview room. The cross-examination by Roberts was brutal, exposing every vague detail in Camb's account and using it against him (see *Chapter 8*). In his re-examination by Casswell, Camb stated he was trying artificial respiration the minute before Steer arrived at the cabin, and Gay Gibson was in no state to ring the bells.

Casswell conspicuously omitted to ask Camb where he was positioned in the cabin at this critical time.

Evelyn Armour stated she was a junior officer in the ATS in early July 1946, when she was called to attend to Private Gibson in her London digs. Gay was lying on the bed with an arched back, her breathing was laboured and her tongue forced to the back of her throat. An ambulance was called and Gay went to the casualty receiving station. There was no record of the admission, but Armour stated this was not unusual if the condition was not serious or did not require further treatment. When Armour next saw her several months later, Gay had lost weight and was considerably thinner.

Peter Dalby stated he met Gay Gibson in January 1946. He described her as "very hysterical" and an "excitable neurotic". He said that during the overseas tour of *The Man with a Load of Mischief*, she had become infatuated with a lorry driver within a matter of days. He also told of a "hysterical fit" when they toured Wales in December 1946. Under cross-examination from Roberts, Dalby confirmed that the troupe was on tour in southern England from 23 June 1946, not returning to London until 3 August 1946.

If he was correct, Evelyn Armour could not have attended to Gay in early July 1946. However, when re-examined by Casswell, Armour identified Private Gibson from Gay's photograph, and Roberts never pursued the point.

Roland Soper, marine surveyor, had measured the distance of the route Steer said he took when he was summoned to cabin 126. Including the two short flights of steps to ascend from A to B Deck, it was 54 yards. This took 63 seconds to walk at an ordinary pace and just 25 seconds walking briskly.

If it took Steer three or four minutes to reach cabin 126, as he claimed originally, he could not have left A Deck immediately on hearing the bells, or he briefly went somewhere else before visiting the cabin.

Mike Abel, salesman and amateur actor, lived in Johannesburg and met Gay at the end of July 1947 for the rehearsals of *Golden Boy*. Gay told him that she had come to South Africa because of her health – she had a chest complaint and mentioned asthma. She fainted in Abel's car and he noticed her lips were bluish. He was present when she fainted on two further occasions, at which times other cast members were also present. She was very charming but would start laughing or crying hysterically for no reason. About mid-August, Gay asked Abel for £200 so she could travel to England because she was pregnant. He refused.

According to Doreen Mantle, Gay accused Mike Abel of making her pregnant; she was concerned her period was late. If the couple had been intimate, it happened very quickly, unless she had met Abel before being cast in Golden Boy.

Henry Gilbert, hairdresser and producer of *Golden Boy*, said Gay was charming but highly strung. Gay told him she was in love with Mike Abel, but he saw no signs to confirm this. On another occasion, crying, she told him cryptically that she "could not love like other girls". Gay said she came to South Africa because of her health – asthma – and he observed she was often tired at the end of rehearsals. One evening, he recalled, Gay fainted in a busy Johannesburg street in front of the entire cast.

Dr Ena Schoub, medical practitioner and Gilbert's wife, met Gay at the end of July 1947, after she was cast in *Golden Boy*. She accompanied Gay to a fitness club on several occasions, and noticed that Gay tired easily, became breathless and had to discontinue the exercises. Gay told the doctor she was sexually experienced and was anxious about a two-week late period. Schoub asked whether she had taken precautions. Gay looked blankly at the doctor, who advised using a diaphragm contraceptive.

Dr Frederick Hocking, pathologist, found evidence of urine on the top sheet, presumed to be from the deceased. There was no blood present in the sample, suggesting there was no rape. He agreed that blood in saliva and the passing of urine was consistent with strangulation, but they were also consistent with death from natural causes. In fact, he thought blood in saliva was less likely with strangulation. The sudden stiffening and relaxation of the body he thought was more consistent with heart failure preceded by lung congestion. He stated that the injuries on Camb's forearm were far too deep to be self-inflicted by scratching. He concluded that death by strangulation and by natural causes were both possibilities, but neither one could be said to be more probable than the other.

Fourth Day: Monday 22 March 1948
The Case for the Defence (continued)

Professor James Webster, forensic pathologist, stated that a natural death as described by the prisoner could have occurred. He suggested there were four possible causes of natural sudden death in this case: the bursting of a brain aneurism; indirect heart failure, typically an infection of the heart by a septic focus elsewhere in the body; direct heart failure through heart disease; and an asthmatic attack. In the professor's opinion, each was as likely as strangulation. An asthmatic attack could cause symptoms associated with failing circulation – typically bluish colouring in the lips and nails. Fainting and bluish lips and nails would be consistent with a heart problem In his experience, the scratches were too far up Camb's forearm to be typical of strangulation, but he could not rule it out.

The Closing Speeches

In closing for the defence, Joshua Casswell summarised all the points in favour of his client's innocence: Gay must have known why a man was coming to her cabin so late at night, and she apparently let him enter; the contraceptive showed she was sexually active; and her health problems, particularly her weak chest and fainting attacks, meant death by natural causes could not be ruled out. He reinforced this last point by highlighting the testimony of the two experts, Hocking and Webster. He also argued that there was insufficient time for the prisoner to throttle the young woman. This argument was premised on the fact that Steer said he arrived at the cabin within a minute. He also stressed that Camb was unaware the bells had been rung. If he had realised, he could have easily bolted the door, or slipped unnoticed from the cabin. He also said that Camb could have easily told falsehoods to make his story more convincing but refused to do so. He was now telling the truth.

Prosecutor Geoffrey Roberts reminded the jury that Camb had lied repeatedly for a week. He only changed his story after Herbert Gibbons informed him that the police were satisfied that he was in the cabin at the critical time, and denials of this fact would prejudice any other explanation he might advance later. Roberts batted away the testimony concerning Gay's health by pointing out that she was passed fit by an army medical, during which there was no mention of asthma or cardiac problems. He was scornful of expert opinion suggesting Gay might have caused the forearm injuries in a death grasp, while the prisoner denied she had injured him in any way. The missing black pyjamas were evidence that no intimacy took place, and the ringing of both bells evidence that Camb's advances were unwelcome.

The Summing Up

Mr Justice Hilbery carefully examined the evidence of the case, although from the defence's perspective it was largely the prosecution's case. Even when the judge believed Camb was telling the truth, the prisoner's words were used against him. For example, the judge correctly pointed out that, according to Camb, Gay never explicitly invited him to her cabin, making it unlikely that his advances were welcome. However, as Casswell had pointed out, it would have been easy for Camb to fabricate such an invitation during his testimony. He could not have been contradicted and it might have engendered doubt in the minds of the jury. Possibly by chance rather than judgement, the judge's final topic was the black pyjamas, which seemed to only stress the importance of the missing garments.

His words echoed around the Great Hall and in the minds of the jury as they retired to consider their verdict. They returned after only 45 minutes.

The Verdict
The foreman announced that the jury had unanimously found the prisoner guilty of murder. The clerk of the assize invited James Camb to make a brief statement on why the court should not pass a judgement of death. Camb stated, "My lord, at the opening of this case I was asked to plead guilty or not guilty. I pleaded not guilty, and I repeat that statement now."

The Sentence
Mr Justice Hilbery told the prisoner that he would "be taken hence to a lawful prison, and thence to a place of execution and that you will be hanged by the neck until you be dead".

Exhibit 9: The Nightwatchman's Walk

How long did it take Fred Steer to reach cabin 126?

In his police statement {*see Exhibit 4*}, Steer said nothing about the time it took him to walk to cabin 126 from the A Deck Pantry, other than he left immediately. However, this is what he later said at the committal hearing:

Steer: You have to go up about a dozen steps and walk about a couple of yards to get from the pantry to the indicator board. It would take longer than half a minute to get from the pantry to the indicator board and then to cabin 126. I would say three or four minutes.
Counsel: You still say three or four minutes is correct?
Steer: Definitely, yes.

Roland Soper, the marine surveyor who later testified at the trial, also gave evidence at the committal. He stated that, at an ordinary pace, it took a minute to walk from the A Deck Pantry to cabin 126 on B Deck, including visiting the indicator board. By the time of the trial, Steer would have known what the surveyor said and changed his mind:

Counsel: I suggest to you that the journey would take you under a minute?
Steer: Yes.
Counsel: At the committal hearing did you not say that it took you three or four minutes to get to the cabin door?
Steer: I did, but I did not take particular notice of the time then. Directly I heard the bell, I went to the cabin as quickly as I could.
Counsel: You do not say now it is three or four minutes, do you, having thought it over?
Steer: Definitely not.

According to the surveyor, at a fast walking pace, it took less than half a minute to reach the cabin. Had Steer made his way immediately and quickly on hearing the bells, it is unlikely he would have opened the door to see Camb standing by the chest of drawers. Rather, he would have been attempting to revive Gay (misadventure), assaulting Gay (manslaughter) or strangling her (murder). It is reasonable to assume that Steer did not leave immediately, instead delaying his departure by two or three minutes. A delay in responding is consistent with the testimony of his superior, James Murray, who said that he instructed Steer to answer the ringing bells. Clearly, this would have been unnecessary if Steer had left directly, as he claimed.

Exhibit 10: Gay's Last Letter

Dated just four days before she died, Gay's letter below is the last to her parents, and possibly the last she ever wrote.

Union-Castle Line

R. M. M. V. "Durban Castle"

Monday 13 October 1947

Dearest Mums and Dads,

I suppose one could almost call this vessel a "ghost ship"! Actually there is hardly a sign of life anywhere. Personally I spend most of the day dozing, and also being very well looked after.

Today the weather brightened considerably and I spent the morning dozing in the deck-chair. This afternoon I went to bed and had tea brought to my cabin. This evening a cinema show should prove a slight diversion.

I have spoken casually to one or two people. As a matter of fact I am the only "Miss" travelling in first class. My table companions are very congenial and I am so glad that there is not to be all those organised games. Tomorrow we are having a dance on board. This will be the first of three, which I feel is just about right.

I asked the Cumberland Hotel for accommodation and hope to have a definite reply in a few days' time. We dock in Southampton the morning of the 25th which is a Saturday. Apparently there is a boat-train connection which should get me up to London by 1 o'clock. This gives me time to find somewhere to stay – just for a few days of course. Unfortunately, it will be a Saturday, which is terribly busy in London.

Give my love to Joe and Auntie Lena. I will write them soon.

Wish you could share this comfort with me.

Your loving Eileen.

Exhibit 11: The Three Affidavits

The following extracts are taken from the original, signed affidavits that were handed to Southampton CID by South African police. This is the first time the women's actual words have been published. They are reproduced in chronological order by date of the alleged incident. All three affidavits were signed 5 November 1947. To protect the identities of those directly involved, I have used their initials only.

AFFIDAVIT A was made by Miss A, a nanny who had travelled on the *Durban Castle* with her employer to South Africa. The statement was made in Cape Town and sworn in the presence of the local Commissioner of Oaths.

Date and time: Thursday 18 September 1947, 10:30pm.
Location: Deck Chair Locker, Promenade Deck.
Camb had arranged to meet this young woman on Promenade Deck. When she arrived, he told her to go to "the cabin where he kept his deck equipment". Camb followed, bringing two drinks.

"Camb locked the door of the deckchair cabin and we sat down on deckchairs. Camb sat next to me. We talked pleasantly for a while before Camb went to fetch more drinks… He came to me and wanted to kiss me, but I would not let him. I then said that I must leave, as I realised I should not be there. Camb said I should kiss him before I left, but I refused.

"The next thing I remember is that I was in a kneeling position on the floor with my back against the seat of the chair and the back of my neck on the deck chair. Camb was kneeling by me. He had one hand on my throat, strangling me, and his other hand was around the back of my neck. He was pressing my head down on the chair. Everything happened suddenly and I do not remember how I came to be in that position.

"Camb eventually released me. I was practically hysterical. There was blood from my mouth on the collar of his white jacket. His face was dripping with perspiration. Camb said he hoped for my sake as well as his that I would not say anything. He said he could not understand what came over him. He said he was sorry."

According to the affidavit, Miss A went back to her cabin immediately. She looked in the mirror: her face was purple and the whites of her eyes were red. The next day her eyes were still bloodshot, so she wore sunglasses to hide the fact. She initially told a friend she had fallen down the stairs before confiding in her what had actually happened. She continued:

"Three days later I went and saw the ship's doctor. I told him someone had tried to strangle me on the first-class deck and informed him I was using Optrex for my eyes, and the doctor said it was all right, but my eyes would not clear up for a month. I later showed Camb my eyes, and he said, 'Good God! I did not think your eyes would come up like that.' I spoke to Camb once or twice after that."

Corroboration: It is not known whether the ship's doctor confirmed the conversation, nor do we know whether he enquired further about the strangulation. However, a children's nurse and acquaintance of the victim, said she had been told of the attack. In her statement to the South African police, she said, "During the afternoon of 18 September 1947, my friend informed me that she had an appointment with James Camb that evening. The following morning she came into my cabin wearing dark glasses. I noticed her eyes were bloodshot and there was discolouration in her face. She told me that she had been out the previous night on the deck with James Camb and that he tried to strangle her."

AFFIDAVIT B was made by Miss B, a British woman who had travelled on the *Durban Castle* with her aunt, who occupied a separate cabin. The statement was made in Johannesburg and sworn in the presence of the local Commissioner of Oaths.

Date and time: Sunday 21 or Monday 22 September 1947, 2:30pm.
Location: B Deck.

"I went to my cabin to have a rest at approximately 2:30pm. I shut the door of my cabin, but did not lock it and went to sleep in the dark, as my cabin had no porthole. I fell asleep. Afterwards I suddenly woke and found Jimmy kneeling quietly next to my bed. I immediately got up but, before I could completely rise, Jimmy pushed me back onto my bed holding my shoulder. At the time I wore a pair of grey shorts with shoulder straps and a blouse.

"I then struggled to get up, but did not succeed as Jimmy got on top of me, his whole body covering mine. In view of the weight of this man on top of me, I was unable to shout, and at the same time he held down my shoulders and kissed me. It was all such a shock to me that I cannot remember all that happened. I do remember, however, that he tried to undo the shoulder straps of my shorts. He also pressed my breasts, but I eventually succeeded in pushing him away from me. I told him my aunt was next door to me. This had the desired effect and Jimmy got up, but he forced me down on the bed again. This time I knocked on the wall, and then Jimmy got up and told me to stay as he was going to fetch my tea. He then left my cabin."

Miss B stated that she found the incident embarrassing and, although she told a male acquaintance and the assistant purser, she did not want the captain informed. It is interesting to note that she was on first-name terms with Camb, who she also said was "apt to be forward" with her.

Corroboration: An actuary travelling on the *Durban Castle* stated that Miss B told him of the incident the next day. He provided a statement to the South African police, in which he said, "She told me she had been in her cabin resting and had gone to sleep and woke up to find a man in her cabin who was leaning over her and kissed her."

The purser, John Catterall, confirmed that Miss B visited him at about 4pm on Thursday 18 September to complain about James Camb. This was about an earlier incident that occurred on the same day Miss A (Affidavit A) was attacked. Catterall told police, "She told me that just previously, on the day, she had been going down to her cabin when she was followed by a deck steward, whom she described. She also said he had tried to follow her into her cabin. He tried to get hold of her but she had pushed him away, and came immediately to the purser's office to report the matter."

AFFIDAVIT C was made by Miss C, a British girl who was living with her parents in Durban at the time. She had travelled with her parents on the *Durban Castle* for a holiday in Cape Town. The statement was made in Durban and sworn in the presence of the local Commissioner of Oaths.

Date and time: Tuesday 7 October 1947, 12:30am .
Location: B Deck.
James Camb had talked to Miss C on at least two occasions during the voyage. At 11pm, 6 October 1947, during a dinner dance, Camb approached an officer who was dancing with her and told him to make it the last dance, claiming the band wanted to retire. She then departed for her cabin, undressed and went to bed.

"I did not lock my cabin door, but switched off the light. I awoke at about 12:30am and saw the steward [identified as James Camb] standing next to my bed. He told me he was sorry that he had to stop the dance as the officers were not allowed to dance with passengers. I told him that he was not allowed to be in my cabin either, but he just laughed and sat down at the end of my bed. He then put his arm around me and put his face next to my cheek. I asked him to go but he took no notice. He started to kiss me and I attempted to push him away, but he still held onto me.

"He remained in my cabin for about 20 minutes. He did not make any indecent suggestions, neither did he indecently touch me, but he kissed me about three or four times. I turned my back towards him and buried my face in my pillow. He remained sitting on my bed for a while. He then got up, switched off the light, closed my door and left. I did not scream as I was not afraid of him."

Miss C stated that she attempted to tell the officer from the dinner dance that Camb was in her cabin that night but she was interrupted and never finished the conversation, nor did she tell anyone else. It appears that this witness was approached by the South African police as part of the investigation.

Corroboration: None.

Camb's behaviour in Affidavits B and C was similar: he went uninvited to a young woman's cabin, made unwanted advances, and eventually left. Affidavit A shows markedly different behaviour: the incident occurred in a locked equipment store on Promenade Deck; the attack was violent; and the victim returned to her cabin (two decks down) after the attack.

The most violent attack of the three occurred first. Did Camb tone down his aggression after this incident, or was it just a matter of time before his violence erupted again?

Exhibit 12: The Accountant's Conversation

According to a rumour at the time of the trial, Gay's missing black pyjamas were left in the room of another passenger, a professional man. According to the report below, the rumour was true: they were in the cabin of a dentist travelling first class. After checking the facts, there is nothing in the report to suggest that the accountant – who reported the story to police – fabricated it, and its central allegation could not be disproved. As the accountant was accused of "suffering from some slight mental disorder" without this being verified, his name and address has been redacted.

GLOUCESTERSHIRE CONSTABULARY
Cheltenham Station, 24 May 1948
Subject: Murder of Eileen Gibson

I respectfully report that at 8.30pm on Friday 21 May, the Witness [real name redacted], age 34, an accountant, called at this office and stated that during the evening of Monday 17 May, he was in the "Bull Hotel", Peterborough, when he got into conversation with Mr John Langham of the Progress Report Staff, BBC, London. The Witness states they were discussing the question of capital punishment when the conversation turned to the case of James Camb who was convicted of the murder of Eileen Gibson.

The Witness asserts that Langham told him that he had seen the black pyjamas that had figured so prominently in the case, only five days previously, they having been shown to him by his (Langham's) dentist who practises in Cavendish Square, London.

The dentist is purported to have told Langham that he returned to England on the same ship as Eileen Gibson and occupied the cabin next to hers. They became friendly and on the night before the murder, she slept with him in his cabin, leaving behind the black pyjamas. He did not report these facts to the police for fear of repercussions the publicity would have on his practice and private life.

The Witness was not able to give the name of the dentist or the private address of Langham, but stated the latter could be obtained from the Hotel Register at the "Bull Hotel", Peterborough.

I have made enquiries respecting the background of the Witness and have ascertained that he is known to the Cirencester Police, in which district his father resides. He is well educated and converses rationally, but is thought to be suffering from some slight mental disorder. In March 1941 he was interviewed in this town respecting the theft of a pedal bicycle, but the evidence was insufficient to justify the charge.

On 30 September, 1941, he appeared at Gloucester Magistrates' Court charged with larceny from his lodgings and was bound over for two years.

He is leaving this district on 29 May, when his address will be [address redacted] in Peterborough.

I respectfully suggest that a copy of this report be forwarded to the chief constable, Southampton, for his information and any action he considers necessary.

Signed, Albert J. Barker, Detective Constable.

Received Southampton CID 25 May 1948.
Signed by Detective Sergeant Quinlan, 26 May 1948.

Exhibit 13: Panic Porthole

Less than three weeks after his release from prison on licence, James Camb's story was serialised in the *Sunday Pictorial*. Based on his notes, the five ghost-written articles provide his final word on the case.

The week before the first article was published, an advertisement for the series appeared in national and local press. It promised much:

James Camb was sentenced to death for the murder of the strange and beautiful Gay Gibson on the liner Durban Castle. He was reprieved and served a "life" sentence. He has just been released. Now he makes an amazing admission to the Sunday Pictorial.

– He claims that he did not tell the whole truth when he was charged with Gay's death

– He says quite frankly that he lied and held back vital evidence at his trial

– He admits that his greatest mistake was to push Gay's body through the porthole and deny the real truth of his love-making with her

– His new evidence, which was not given in court, will enable readers of the Sunday Pictorial to answer the question – How did Gay Gibson really die?

A salacious story combining sex and death could only be good for business. And the *Sunday Pictorial* needed to attract new readers to justify the £2,500 it had paid Camb to serialise the story. It was a large sum, equivalent to £50,000 in cash today but equal to the average house price in the UK at the time.

In fact, the five articles provided no new evidence, but there were three major changes to Camb's story compared to his trial testimony: the scratches on his body were inflicted by Gay Gibson as she died in his arms; he thought he had been recognised by Steer; and, echoing the closing speech of Casswell, he rang the cabin bells by accident.

The second article, 'Panic Porthole', provides "the truth" about the fateful events inside cabin 126. Published on 4 October 1959, it is reproduced below with permission of Trinity Mirror Group. It should be stressed again that the journalist's priority was to create a dramatic story with evocative language, and would have paid less attention to detail. In addition, Camb was released from prison on licence, meaning he had to show good behaviour, otherwise he could find himself incarcerated again. It was not in his interest to admit that any salacious or violent behaviour had occurred. My comments are italicised and in parentheses.

Sunday Pictorial, 4 October 1959

Panic Porthole

How Gay Gibson died by James Camb

Edited by Harry Ashbrook

Our two half-smoked cigarettes lay in an ashtray beside the bunk in cabin 126 as I took the lovely Gay Gibson in my arms. She whispered, "Jimmy, Jimmy." It was the first time she had called me by my name. I felt relaxed and happy as the moonlight flooded through the open porthole. At that moment I had no premonition of the horror that was to come – for Gay Gibson was to die in my arms that night.

What I am telling you is the real truth of what happened – the real truth about how she died. I lied when I was tried for her murder. Those lies nearly took me to the gallows. Now I am a free man again after nearly twelve years in jail, I am telling my story for the first time. When I have finished, the Sunday Pictorial will present further arguments for and against me. Then you can judge whether I was guilty.

As I told you last week, I was a steward on the liner *Durban Castle*, homeward bound from Cape Town, when I met Gay Gibson, a first-class passenger. She was bored. I was restless. And when she seemed to want me to visit her cabin, I took the opportunity.

This was not my first affair with a woman passenger. I was wary and cautious. Deliberately, I left the door unlocked in case of trouble. There had been complaints about me before. On the outward voyage to Cape Town there had been an incident when a young girl invited me down to her cabin and exasperated me by her teenage behaviour. (*This might be a reference to AJ, Affidavit C*). I put her over my knee and gave her a good spanking.

But with Gay Gibson I felt safe. I thought she was a woman of the world and understood my intentions. So, as I pulled her almost roughly towards me and kissed the nape of her neck, I had second thoughts about the cabin door. Perhaps it would be better if I locked it. I made a move to do so, telling Gay it would be safer.

She smiled and said, "It doesn't matter, nobody will come in. We will be quite safe." Those were the last words she ever spoke. And they will live in my mind until I die.

I returned to her bunk and time came to a halt. Gay began to moan as I clasped her to me. She gripped my arms; her nails dug into my flesh (*something he flatly denied at the trial*). But I felt no pain. It never occurred to me that she was resisting my advances. (*This might be a clumsy way of saying, "I knew she would not resist me" or a Freudian slip that she had resisted his advances*).

Then something happened – something I will never understand. And will never forget. Suddenly, her whole body stiffened in my arms. Her back arched in a violent spasm. (*He did not say this at his trial, but would have heard Evelyn Armour's testimony*). She heaved a long, tired sigh and her head lolled awkwardly to one side. Her eyes opened wide and fixed me with a sightless stare.

This was the moment of my supreme terror. I jumped off the bed, trembling. I thought – what in God's name have I done to this poor girl? I leaned against the dressing table (*chest of drawers*), gripping the sides hard, trying to collect my thoughts. (*Steer said that when he pushed open the door, he saw Camb leaning against the chest of drawers*). I was like a man standing in a long, dark tunnel. I could see no light. No hope.

Desperately I searched my mind. Had I done anything that could have caused her death? I looked at my hands. There was no sign of blood. I could not understand it. Unsteadily, I returned to the bunk. I gazed at the body of Gay Gibson. She lay crookedly across the bed like a broken doll. I was afraid to touch her. Then I felt her pulse. There was nothing. I felt for her heartbeat. But there was no sign of life.

The cabin seemed to swim before me. I began to shake her but her body was still rigid in my hands. (*At his trial he stated her body went limp immediately after Gay heaved under him*). I slapped her face, called her name. But there was no response. All life had gone from her. I stood utterly alone in that swaying cabin, the sweat cold on my back, my mind a swirling storm of fears and unmentionable dreads.

When I stood in court on trial for the murder of Gay I was repeatedly asked this question: "Why didn't you call a doctor?" I did not give a satisfactory answer in court. And I cannot give a satisfactory one now. I can only tell the truth. When I feared Gay Gibson was dead, I panicked. I lost all sense of reality. I thought she was dead, but somewhere in the back of my mind I thought I could bring her back to life. I could not accept the reality of death. I could not believe that death could come so quietly.

Although I had been at sea all my life, I knew very little about artificial respiration. I tried to bring life back to her body. I knelt over her and with my palm downwards I pressed her chest in a slow rhythm, trying to pump air into her. I told the court I went on doing this for 25 minutes. Looking back on it now, I cannot say whether this is true. It could have been five minutes or 500. I was living every second in terror. I noticed a slight froth forming at her lips. Was it a sign she was coming back to life? Or did it mean she was finally dead? I did not know.

Then came a tap on the door. The cabin bells had been rung. The nightwatchman was outside. As he opened the door I rushed to close it. I locked it behind me and said, "All right." Now I saw the reality and understood for the first time the real danger I was in. I thought the nightwatchman would report the incident to the officers on the bridge. Everything was at stake: my job, my family, my future happiness. Although I knew the nightwatchman had not seen the body on the bunk, and had not had much chance to see me, I feared he might have recognised my voice. (*At his trial he said he was confident he had not been recognised*).

I knew I had very little time. Once again I went back to the bunk. Gay Gibson's body seemed less rigid, and I tried once again to bring her to life. All the time I was pressing my hands onto her chest, I was thinking of the nightwatchman reporting to the bridge. In my terror, I asked: "Who rang the bells?" I knew it could not have been Gay because she was either dead or unconscious when the bells were rung. I said in court that I had no recollection of ringing them myself because I did not call for help. How then did it happen? When I was asked this in court I could give no adequate answer. I had told so many lies when I was first questioned that I felt it was too late to tell the truth. But the truth is that I must have rung them – by accident (*something he flatly denied at his trial*). I believe my hand pressed against the bell push when I turned on the full cabin lights. (*The switch for the main light was not positioned near the bell pushes; the top button was for the cylindrical bed light which was already illuminated*).

If I had told these simple truths in court I believe I would not have been convicted of the murder of Gay Gibson. And now to the last question – why did I bundle the body of Gay Gibson through the porthole? I have no simple answer to this terrifying question. I can only tell you what happened and of the chaotic thoughts that flashed through my bruised and torn mind.

I felt truly and deeply sorry for the woman who had walked so tragically into my life. But I realised there was little I could do. My mind had been poisoned by unknown fears. I stood over her dead body. A cool breeze wafted in through the open porthole. At that moment I realised the porthole was my only escape. I was prepared to take the chance that I had not been recognised by the nightwatchman.

I stood in the middle of the cabin, in my vest and blue trousers, saying aloud to myself, "I've got to get rid of her body. It's my only chance." It never occurred to me that I was throwing away the only evidence that could have saved me from the death cell. I moved to lift Gay from the bunk. She was heavy in my arms. The yellow-flowered dressing gown still hung from her shoulders. Her feet were bare. Her body sagged over my shoulders. Unsteadily, I edged towards the porthole. This was the moment of final decision. I noticed her body was now limp. I stopped and tested her pulse for life. There was no response.

I stumbled as I rested her shoulders on the porthole ledge. I was breathless with fear and exhaustion. The cool breeze from the porthole cut across my face. My knees felt weak and I feared I was going to faint. I bit my lips until they bled. (*The ship's doctor did not note this injury the following day*). The body was swaying in the porthole. I slipped again and began to murmur to myself, "You won't do it… you won't do it…"

Then I thought I heard a sudden noise at the door. I made one last effort and her body slithered through the porthole. I saw the white gleam of her legs as she fell. The moon now seemed a million miles away. There was no splash as the body hit the water.

Exhibit 14: The Sid James Affair

Sid James (born Solomon Joel Cohen, 8 May 1913) was a famous comedy actor, best known for his starring roles in the bawdy *Carry On* films. Born in South Africa, he emigrated with his pregnant wife to England in 1946 to further his acting career. According to his biographer, Cliff Goodwin, there was another reason he left South Africa: he was escaping the infatuation of an obsessive lover who threatened both his marriage and his career. Sid had been seduced and then pursued by a hedonistic, younger woman who had refused to accept that the affair was over. The name of the lover: Eileen 'Gay' Gibson.

According to Goodwin, when the *Durban Castle* docked at Southampton on 25 October 1947, local police searched Gay's suitcases and discovered two diaries and a bundle of letters. Goodwin states these pornographic ramblings revealed that she was returning to England to track down an ex-lover. These were evidently clear enough to identify Sid James, because the Southampton police asked Scotland Yard to question him concerning Gay Gibson's death. A detective sergeant interviewed James in late October. When he was asked whether he knew Eileen Gibson, Sid James is reported to have turned white, gripping the edge of a desk to stop his hands from shaking. He admitted the affair, although we are not told if he said when it occurred, claiming Gay was a nymphomaniac. The police concluded that he had played no part in the death. It appears that Camb's legal team were kept in the dark about this interview, otherwise Sid James would surely have been called as a witness for the defence.

The claim in Goodwin's biography is pertinent because, if true, it would confirm that Gay Gibson was sexually predatory, making it more likely that Camb's attentions were welcomed and less likely that she deliberately pressed the buttons. If she was a nymphomaniac, as James is alleged to have said, she may also have had more than one liaison on board, perhaps accounting for the missing black pyjamas. However, the allegations, as presented in his book, are groundless. Here, I set the record straight.

Goodwin makes several factual assertions concerning Gay and Sid James:

1) Gay's diaries were discovered by police in Gay's cabin

2) Scotland Yard interviewed Sid James

3) Gay Gibson was born in London, spoke with a cockney accent, and was blonde

4) She appeared "to possess a contraceptive in every pocket"

5) The affair occurred in 1946 in Cape Town, and

6) She was returning to England in October 1947 to track down Sid James

If a diary had been found among Gay's possessions, it would have been logged by detectives. In the police files, there is no record of a diary being retrieved from Gay's luggage. Further, despite voluminous correspondence between Southampton CID and the Metropolitan Police on various issues concerning the case, there is no mention of Sid James in any note, letter or communiqué.

Goodwin's description of Gay contains worrying inaccuracies. Gay Gibson was born in India, not London, and grew up in Birkenhead. Although she lived in London for several years while in the ATS, no one who acted with her, or met her on the *Durban Castle*, described her as speaking with a cockney accent. She was a redhead, not a blonde.

The claim that she possessed many contraceptives is at odds with the testimony of Dr Ena Schoub, who stated that Gay seemed ignorant on matters of contraception when she met her several times during the summer of 1947:

Counsel: Did you have any discussion with Miss Gibson about contraceptives?

Schoub: When she told me that her period was overdue, I asked her if she had used a contraceptive. She looked blankly at me. She did not seem to know anything about it and asked me to explain things to her.

The most important assertion from Goodwin is the timing of the affair. In 1946, Gay Gibson was performing with Stars in Battledress. Peter Dalby, a private who worked alongside Gay during this time, testified that he first met Gay in January 1946 during rehearsals for the play *The Man with a Load of Mischief*. After shows in London, it went on tour in England, France and Germany, ending in early August 1946. He testified further that he worked with Gay in a play called *Jane Steps Out*, which had a six-week tour in England from October 1946, and that he had spent much time with her:

Counsel: You were in the same entertainment unit as Miss Gibson for about 12 months?

Dalby: Yes.

Counsel: Was Miss Gibson absent from duty for one day during 1946?

Dalby: No.

During 1946, Gay Gibson worked full-time with an acting troupe that never travelled outside Europe, and she was never noticeably absent from duty. According to Goodwin, however, Gay had been hired by Gwen Ffrangcon-Davies sometime in 1946 after a tour collapsed, leaving her stranded in Cape Town. This is when the alleged affair with Sid James began. Not only was Gay performing with Stars in Battledress during the whole of 1946 but, according to one of Gay's letters to her mother, she first met Ffrangcon-Davies in Pretoria on 5 April 1947.

According to Goodwin, Sid James left South Africa in the second week of December 1946, arriving at Southampton on Christmas Day. Interestingly, a search of inbound passenger records found no confirmation of this. There is a record, however, of an actor called

Sidney James arriving on the *Carnarvon Castle* at Southampton on 2 November 1946. The passenger was 33 years-old (the age of Sid James at the time) and had travelled from Cape Town accompanied by his wife, who was named as Meggie, aged 33. Married in 1943, Meg James was Sidney's second wife. She was three months younger than him. There can be little doubt that this is the future *Carry On* actor. It establishes the only concrete, albeit tenuous, connection between him and Gay Gibson: they both had sailed on the *Carnarvon Castle*, the liner that took Gay and her mother to South Africa three months later.

A sexual affair needs many things, not least the people concerned being in the same country. Gay was not in South Africa during 1946. Therefore, the specific claims in the book are false. Further, as there is no suggestion that Gay and Sid met during the few months when they were actually residing in the same country, the allegation of an affair is groundless.

The cover of *The Girl in the Stateroom* by Charles Boswell and Lewis Thompson, a book about the trial of James Camb published in America in 1951, shows a redheaded woman seductively lounging on a cabin bed. Above, reads the headline: "She was the desire of all men and all men were her desire." The alleged affair with Sid James fits neatly into this narrative, but it is salacious speculation, taking us further from the truth rather than closer to it.

Note: The allegations can be found in *Sid James: A Biography*, by Cliff Goodwin (2001), pp. 59 to 70.

ACT THREE

The Verdict

You have read the story.
You have sifted the evidence.
Here is my view on what
happened in cabin 126.

The Verdict

MY JUDGEMENT

How did Gay Gibson most likely die? There are three possible verdicts: misadventure, manslaughter and murder. The time has come for me to give my opinion.

James Camb was a smooth-talker and friendly with Gay – points not in dispute. At his trial, the defence argued that he was invited into Gay's cabin late at night because she was amenable to his advances. But a proponent of misadventure cannot have it both ways: one cannot assert that her friendliness resulted in Gay responding to his advances but deny it could also have been exploited by Camb to gain access to her cabin to launch a sexual assault. I do not believe this is a point in favour of any theory.

Camb sustained suspicious injuries on his body, particularly on his right forearm, but the lack of typical defensive injuries on his hands modestly decreases the probability of murder. The presence of urine, believed to be a terminal act, is strongly associated with strangulation, but not uniquely. I believe the urine modestly increases the probability of murder. I suggest the two cancel each other out.

The fact that Camb was in Gay's cabin when the bell-pushes were pressed demands an explanation. I do not believe he pressed them. If he had done so to deliberately seek help, and quickly changed his mind, he would have bolted the cabin door to stop the nightwatchman entering. If he pushed them inadvertently without noticing, he would have figured out how it happened retrospectively. He never did. In fact, when questioned on this point, Camb effectively shrugged his shoulders, and never provided an adequate explanation. His later account in the *Sunday Pictorial* of pressing them accidentally when he turned on the main cabin light cannot be true. That switch was not located by the bedside panel.

Therefore, it is clear to me that Gay rang the bells. If Camb observed the buttons being pressed, he knew the nightwatchman was coming to the cabin, and possibly in short order. Surely, his fear of being discovered in the cabin would have led him to either exit the cabin immediately, or to bolt the door. He did neither. The suggestion that he strangled Gay, and then leaned against the chest of drawers, as if waiting for the nightwatchman to arrive, is implausible.

I believe Camb was unaware that Gay pushed the buttons. It is possible that she flung her right arm out to the side and backwards during the heat of passion, but unlikely. She hit the two buttons either intentionally to summon help, or unintentionally while trying to grab an improvised weapon from the chest of drawers. Either way, his advances were not welcome.

It is a troubling coincidence that Gay's pyjamas also went missing on the night of her death. The simplest explanation is that she was wearing them, but Camb failed to realise because he did not unzip her dressing gown. Had the story of the dentist's pyjamas surfaced before the trial, or was corroborated by others, it would have more credibility. As it stands, I believe the missing pyjamas, like the ringing of the bells, count against misadventure.

The prosecution claimed the most damning evidence against Camb was that he pushed her body through the porthole. Indeed, the strongest motivation for taking this extreme course of action, which was no easy task, was if Gay's lifeless body showed telltale signs of strangulation. His actions after her death point away from misadventure.

Even without the affidavits of the three young women, the circumstantial evidence is stacked against misadventure. I do not believe Camb's story. He was increasingly unable to control his sexual desire for young women, and was swarming around teenagers like a wasp around lemonade. It was only a matter of time before something went terribly wrong. It did, at 3am on 18 October 1947. But was it manslaughter rather than murder?

The affidavits can be interpreted to support either verdict. Camb did not inflict bodily harm when he visited the cabins of the two young women on B Deck (Affidavits B and C), and on both occasions he did not bolt the cabin door. Gay Gibson's cabin was in the same section of B Deck and her door was also left unbolted. By contrast, in the Deckchair Locker on Promenade Deck, Camb bolted the door (Affidavit A). Perhaps this was because he was expecting his advances to be welcomed and did not want any interruptions. Whatever the reason, when he was refused, his alleged reaction was venomous and life-threatening.

I believe there is one decisive factor that differentiates between the two remaining verdicts: Gay's health. She appeared fatigued, reflected by the concern of the *Golden Boy* cast that she might not be able to continue in the play. She fainted on numerous occasions, with her mouth, hands and nails turning blue. She suffered asthma-like symptoms and had "a weak chest". She appeared to be in poor health to all those acting with her in Johannesburg, but the three South African witnesses who testified on this matter were not believed. Doreen Mantle, the last living person to have acted with Gay Gibson, confirms what they said. I believe the simplest explanation for all these symptoms is congenital heart disease.

I believe the following scenario is the most consistent with the available evidence. Camb sexually assaulted Gay Gibson in a similar way to that described in Affidavit B: he got on top of Gay while she was wearing her nightclothes. Unnoticed by him, she hit both buttons with her hand as she struggled against him. In the stultifyingly hot cabin, his body weight pressed down on her, causing breathing difficulties and ultimately triggering heart failure. This is more likely if the assault was prolonged for several minutes, and I strongly suspect the nightwatchman never arrived at the cabin within a minute, as he claimed.

After Gay expired, Camb jumped up, stunned. He did not know what had happened or what to do. He leaned back against the chest of drawers, working out his best course of action, when the cabin door started to open. He slammed it shut. Worried he might have been seen, Camb was now trapped by his own reprehensible behaviour and reputation. What could he say, and who would believe him? If the body was discovered, he feared he would lose his career at sea, and so he callously disposed of it through the porthole.

Consistent with his other alleged sexual assaults, he did not remove Gay's clothes, and so was unaware that she was wearing her black pyjamas. He later claimed she was wearing nothing under her dressing gown to make it appear that she was anticipating sex. It was one of many lies. After all, he could not reveal the truth without condemning himself.

This account also explains why Camb maintained his innocence. As far as he was concerned, he had not killed Gay. "Does this mean I murdered her?" he asked Detective Sergeant Gibbons. "My God, I did not think it would be as serious as this."

But it was that serious. James Camb had killed Gay Gibson, albeit unintentionally. So my verdict is:

Manslaughter – Gay Gibson died suddenly during a sexual assault by James Camb.

I believe justice was done. James Camb did not deserve to die for his crime, but the prison sentence he served was due not to the competence of the British judicial system, but sheer luck.

"I feel I should not have been found guilty," Camb said in the final *Sunday Pictorial* article in October 1959, "but I have served my sentence, and the debt – whether owed or not – is paid in full." This was hardly a defiant cry of innocence from someone battling to clear his name, but the guilty submission of a deck steward who knew he was responsible for the death of an actress.

OTHER VERDICTS

The following brief overview provides my thoughts on the major books and articles published on the case, listed chronologically. They are all out of print. Where appropriate, the conclusion of the author is stated.

Clark, Geoffrey. Trial of James Camb (1949)
Part of the *Notable British Trials* series, this is the most complete account of the trial. It includes a comprehensive introduction by Clark, who was one of the prosecution lawyers at the trial, and an edited transcript of the failed appeal. This is a must-read book for any criminologist researching the case.

Boswell and Thompson. The Girl in the Stateroom (1951)
This US publication has the cover of a cheap erotic novel. A picture of a seductive-looking redhead, in stockings and with cigarette in hand, reclines on a cabin bed. "She was the desire of all men and all men were her desire" the coverline screams out. The copy on the back proclaims, "the law ripped apart her most intimate affairs to find her killer". Utter nonsense. Readers expecting something salacious would have been extremely disappointed. The book is similar to Geoffrey Clark's *Trial of James Camb*: it provides an edited transcript of the trial. Boswell and Thompson provide colourful descriptions of the goings-on inside the courtroom, and there is a brief description of the affidavits against Camb, which they believe clinch his guilt.
Conclusion: Guilty of murder.

Humphreys, Travers. Rex v James Camb (1953)
Humphreys was one of the three judges who heard, and dismissed, James Camb's appeal, which accounts for the rather odd title of

this article. According to Humphreys, there was only one issue to be decided by the jury at the trial: did Camb silence Gay Gibson after he forced his attentions on her or "did she die from some mysterious, unexpected but natural cause" (here the word "mysterious" has connotations of "doubtful"). This seems plain wrong to me. Surely, the only issue for the jurors was whether the prosecution had proved beyond reasonable doubt that Camb had murdered her. Was there sufficient circumstantial evidence to meet this burden of proof? Humphreys does raise his game, presenting an excellent summing-up of the case against Camb, with some concisely made arguments.

Conclusion: Guilty of murder.

Symons, Julian. The Porthole Case (1960)

This is a chapter from his book, *A Reasonable Doubt.* As the title suggests, Symons maintains that Camb should not have been convicted. He claims that Camb was induced to believe that he was welcome in Gay's cabin that night. Once this is accepted, he argues, Camb's version of events is as plausible as that adduced by the prosecution. Symons presents the case for and against Camb, as well as briefly examining the medical evidence that, he concludes, "did not tell strongly either way". His case for Camb rests on the evidence of Gay Gibson's character, her conduct that evening and the timing problem – Camb would have been unable to strangle his victim before Steer arrived.

Conclusion: Not guilty.

Casswell, Joshua. The Porthole Murder (1961)

This is a chapter from his memoirs, *A Lance for Liberty*, which recounts other major trials in which he was involved. It was serialised in a national newspaper in the early 1960s. Casswell believed Camb was innocent and provides a good case for his view

here. Possibly, it is better than his summing up at the trial. With greater time, his argument is honed and delivered more simply than his speech to the jury. It also provides brief glimpses of conversations between counsel and client. It is not a balanced account, however, as it does not weigh up the evidence for his guilt. To the last, Casswell was a counsel for his client.
Conclusion: Not guilty.

Roberts, Geoffrey. The Porthole Murderer (1964)
The next book to reference the case was written by Casswell's adversary at the trial, Khaki Roberts, who included a section on it in his memoirs, *Law and Life*. As the title of the section suggests, Roberts believed that Camb was rightly found guilty and, one suspects, was a little disappointed that he was not hanged. Roberts suggests the three main points of the trial were Gay Gibson's health, her morals and the cause of her death as inferred by the medical experts. Interestingly, for the latter he lists eight items of evidence, yet only one of them is about the physical evidence – the scratches on Camb's forearm, "with their dreadful significance of his victim's dying struggle", which was disputed. He mentions more physical evidence later, particularly the urine on the sheets, which he believed had tended to destroy the case for the defence.
Conclusion: Guilty of murder.

Herbstein, Denis. The Porthole Murder Case (1991)
After Boswell and Thompson, this is the only other book-length treatment of the case, although the author did not have access to the police files. Herbstein interviews contemporary medical experts who provide a more detailed analysis of what could have caused Gay Gibson to die naturally. The central thesis of the book, although it is never explicitly concluded, is that the medical evidence was sufficient to engender reasonable doubt. But did

Herbstein think James Camb most likely murdered Gay Gibson or not? I had the pleasure of speaking to him during the writing of my book and I put this question to him. He did not know.

Conclusion: Guilt not proved beyond a reasonable doubt.

Block and Hostettler. Hanging in the Balance (1997)

This scholarly book tells the story of how Parliament, over the course of two centuries, eventually abolished the death penalty in Britain in 1969. It covers in detail the debates inside and outside of Parliament leading to the temporary suspension of the death penalty in 1948, which allowed James Camb to avoid the gallows.

Research Sources

In researching this book I have relied almost exclusively on primary sources – police reports, witness statements, affidavits, the court transcript and personal correspondence – held by the Hampshire Constabulary History Society. A small subset of these documents, including the three affidavits, is available to view at the National Archive (ref: MEPO 3/2860).

Epilogue

LOST

Victims of notorious murders die twice: once at the hands of their assailants, and once in the eyes of history, their names forever wedded with those of their killers. Even if you believe Gay Gibson was not unlawfully killed, history sees her leading man as James Camb and her stage as the *Durban Castle*. Her real character has been lost, and her reputation traduced, by scurrilous claims and persistent rumours. This seems such a cruel way to remember the potential and expectations of a young life washed away by the indiscriminate tides of misfortune.

Not surprisingly, James Camb lost his marriage. In December 1948, Margaret Camb divorced him on the grounds of adultery, the evidence for which was the testimony given by her husband at his trial. She later married a clerk from the firm of solicitors that had acted on behalf of her former husband.

Described as a "star prisoner", Camb served 11 years of his life sentence before being released on licence in September 1959, aged 42. He changed his surname to Clarke, the middle name of his former wife. He married a barmaid and adopted her young daughter. For a while, it appeared Clarke was lost to the obscurity of an ordinary, decent life, but it did not last. In 1971, an all-too-familiar story was retold. While working at a hotel, he broke into the bedroom of three 11-year-old girls on a school trip. His lewd behaviour was similar to that described in Affidavit B. He was returned to prison to serve out his life sentence and lost his second marriage.

By this time, he had also lost his dashing good looks and easy charm. He was described as a sleazy, dishevelled and irritable old man. He was now a shrivelled husk of his former self and, blaming anyone but himself, felt victimised by the world. He was released from prison in 1978, dying a year later, aged 62. It was a pitiful end to a wasted life.

Two weeks after Camb's appeal in 1948, Joshua Casswell began to suffer heart trouble. He stopped playing golf and was directed to lessen his workload. His final criminal case as a barrister was in December 1950. It ended on a sombre note; he lost the case and his client was hanged. Casswell died in 1963, aged 77. Geoffrey Roberts died four years later, aged 80, having published his memoirs and *Law and Life*, a guide to advocacy, of which he was a fine exponent.

In the ten years following the trial, Daisy Gibson must have felt cursed, or that her faith was being tested more than most. She lost both her remaining children: one was killed in a motorcycle crash and the other died in an accident on an oil rig. Her family had slipped through her fingers like sand, but at least she was able to bury both her boys. Perhaps this provided a measure of peace and closure that she could never obtain with her daughter, forever lost to the deep.

In letters to her daughter, written and posted while Gay was travelling on the *Durban Castle*, Daisy wrote, "I think of you day and night and wish I was nearer." I believe she would have thought about her daughter every day for the rest of her life, possibly tormented by a mother's anguish for letting her travel alone. Daisy died in March 1986. The final stanza of Caroline "Danske" Dandridge's poem *Lost at Sea* seems apposite:

Then my spirit will haste to her resting-place,
As she lies on the wreck-strewn floor;
I will shelter my love in a close embrace
Till the sea shall be no more.

MORE FOR THE COLD CASE JURY

Don't just read about a murder... solve it! For lovers of crime stories, this new collection of Cold Case Jury books will not just bring a murder story to life - it will make you a part of it. Each one tells the story of an unsolved crime in an evocative and compelling way, exposing the strengths and weaknesses of past evidence, presenting new information and asking the reader to come to their own verdict.

THE GREEN BICYCLE MYSTERY
By Antony M Brown

The first in a unique set of books tells the story of the tragic death of Bella Wright in 1919.

In a lonely lane in rural Leicestershire, a solitary bicycle lies on its side, its metal frame catching the glow of the fading evening light. The front wheel slowly turns about its axle, producing a soft clicking; a rhythmic sound, soothing like the ticking of a study clock.

Next to the bicycle, lying at an angle across the road, is a young woman. She is partly on her back, partly on her left side, with her right hand almost touching the mudguard of the rear wheel. Her legs rest on the roadside verge, where fronds of white cow parsley and pink rosebay rise above luxuriant summer foliage. On her head sits a wide-brimmed hat. She is dressed in a blouse and long skirt underneath a light raincoat, the pockets of which contain an empty purse and a box of matches. The blood-flecked coat tells a story...

Coming soon:
MOVE TO MURDER
By Antony M Brown

The puzzling murder of Julia Wallace in Liverpool in 1931. A telephone message is left at a chess club, instructing one of its members, insurance agent William Wallace, to meet a Mr Qualtrough. But the address given by the mystery caller does not exist and Wallace returns home to find his wife Julia bludgeoned to death.

The case turns on the telephone call. Who made it? The police thought it was Wallace, creating an alibi that might have come straight from an Agatha Christie thriller. Others believe Wallace innocent but disagree on the identity of the real murderer. The Cold Case Jury must decide what happened in one of the most celebrated cold cases of all time.

Also by Mirror Books

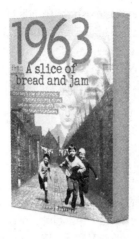

1963 - A Slice of Bread and Jam
Tommy Rhattigan

Tommy lives at the heart of a large Irish family in derelict Hulme in Manchester, ruled by an abusive, alcoholic father and a negligent mother. Alongside his siblings he begs (or steals) a few pennies to bring home to avoid a beating, while looking for a little adventure of his own along the way.

His foul-mouthed and chaotic family may be deeply flawed, but amongst the violence, grinding poverty and distinct lack of hygiene and morality lies a strong sense of loyalty and, above all, survival.

During this single year – before his family implodes and his world changes for ever – Tommy almost falls foul of the welfare officers, nuns, police – and Myra Hindley and Ian Brady.

An adventurous, fun, dark and moving true story of the only life young Tommy knew.

Also by Mirror Books

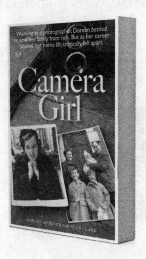

Camera Girl
Doreen Spooner with Alan Clark

The true story of a woman coping with a tragic end to the love of her life, alongside a daily fight to establish herself and support her children.

A moving and inspiring memoir of Doreen Spooner – a woman ahead of her time. Struggling to hold her head high through the disintegration of the family she loves through alcoholism, she began a career as Fleet Street's first female photographer.

While the passionate affair and family life she'd always dreamed of fell apart, Doreen walked into the frantic world of a national newspaper. Determined to save her family from crippling debt, her work captured the Swinging Sixties through political scandals, glamorous stars and cultural icons, while her homelife spiralled further out of control.

The two sides of this book take you through a touching and emotional love story, coupled with a hugely enjoyable portrait of post-war Britain.

Mirror Books

Also by Mirror Books

THE INTERNATIONAL BESTSELLER

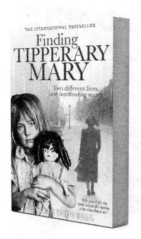

Finding Tipperary Mary
Phyllis Whitsell

The astonishing real story of a daughter's search for her own past
and the desperate mother who gave her up for adoption.

Phyllis Whitsell began looking for her birth mother as a young woman
and although it was many years before she finally met her, their lives had
crossed on the journey without their knowledge.

When they both eventually sat together in the same room,
the circumstances were extraordinary, moving and
ultimately life-changing.

This is a daughter's personal account of the remarkable
relationship that grew from abandonment into love,
understanding and selfless care.

Also by Mirror Books

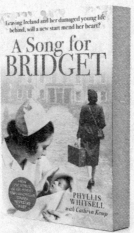

A Song for Bridget
Phyllis Whitsell

The heartbreaking prequel to the Sunday Times Bestseller, 'Finding Tipperary Mary'.

At aged 15 Bridget discovers the body of her kindly stepfather who has hanged himself. After her mother's death, Bridget finds love with a local lad, Bill. Her brother - now head of the household - discovers the relationship, stops it, threatens Bill and beats and rapes Bridget.

Bill goes to England, while Bridget endures a terrible life at home. After giving birth to her brother's child at a single mother's institution, she has her child removed for adoption and she flees to England in search of Bill and a new life.

However, Bill is now married with a child of his own. They begin an affair but Bill, wracked with guilt, returns to his wife. Now pregnant with Bill's child, Bridget's drinking becomes worse. As her life spirals out of control – her daughter, Phyllis (named after her beloved young half-sister Philomena) is born. Bridget holds onto the child she has had with the love her life for as long as she can – but is finally forced to let her go. Will they ever meet again...?

Also by Mirror Books

Playland
Anthony Daly

The voice of one man from within a dark scandal that nestled in the heart of London's Soho in the 1970s

Travelling to a new city to escape The Troubles in his native Northern Ireland, Tony Daly accepted a job in Foyles Bookshop. However, his naivety saw him fall foul of predators, looking for young men to sexually exploit.

Tony spent years hiding the secret of his abuse at the hands of some of the most influential men in the country. But finally, his lost voice ripped through the safe family life he had built over 40 years.

Stylishly written and politically explosive, this is the haunting true story of a young man's descent into a hell designed to satisfy the powerful. A world which destroyed the lives of everyone involved.

"Tony Daly's horrific story demands to be heard - his journey into the very heart of a corrupt and perverted establishment is simply off the scale ..."

Paul Frift, *Film Maker/Producer ITV's 'Victoria'*

Also by Mirror Books

A Mayfair 100 murder-mystery

Murder in Belgravia
Lynn Brittney

London, 1915. Ten months into the First World War and the City is flooded with women taking over the work vacated by men.

Chief Inspector Peter Beech, a young man invalided out of the war in one of the first battles, is investigating the murder of an aristocrat and the man's wife will only speak to a woman about the unpleasant details of the case. Beech persuades the Chief Commissioner to allow him to set up a clandestine team to deal with this case and pulls together a small crew of hand-picked women and professional policemen. Their telephone number: Mayfair 100.

Delving into the seedier parts of WWI London, the team investigate brothels and criminal gangs and underground drug rings that supply heroin to the upper classes. Will the Mayfair 100 gang solve the murder? If they do, will they be allowed to continue working as a team?

The first in an exciting series of fascinatingly-detailed stories involving the Mayfair 100 crimebusting team working London's streets during the First World War.

Mirror Books